Road to Kasane
Scarleg's Pride
Harvey's Clan
Savuti Channel
Gametrackers
Lloyd's Camp
Camp Clan
Twin Hills Clan
Maome's Pride
N
W
E
S
Tshaba's Pride
Warthog Alley Clan
Eastern Clan
Road to Maun

Savuti

Lion territories
Hyena territories

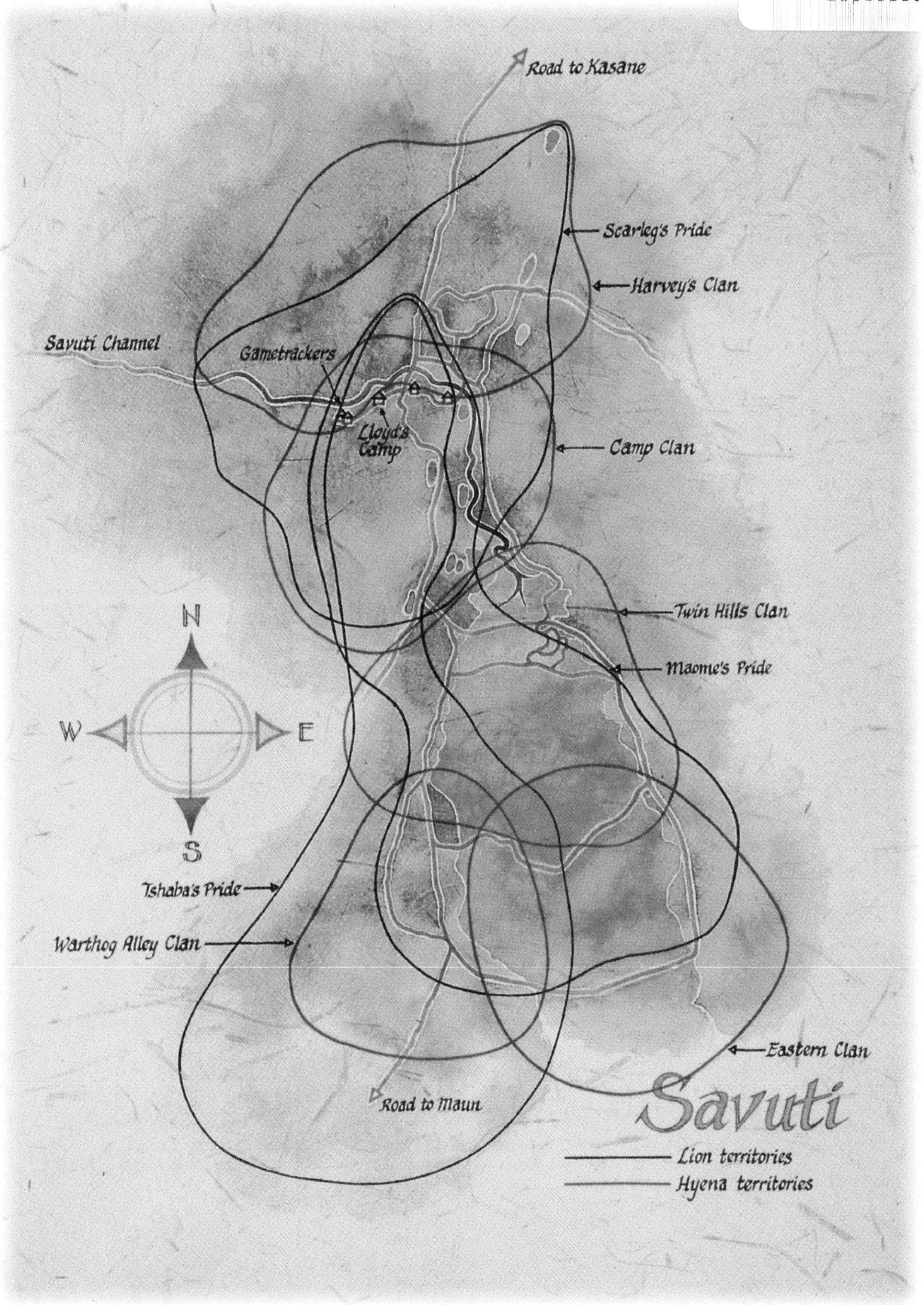

A lioness waits motionless at the Savuti water hole until the impala and kudu she stalks grow accustomed to her silhouette.

Botswana has two seasons: one hot and wet; the other dry and hot during the day, but with near-freezing temperatures at night.

The lioness explodes into fleeing impalas. Her ability to focus all attention on one dodging antelope will determine her success.

Taking to the water, a kudu bull sacrifices its only advantage—speed—and pays the price.

Even in slumber, the importance of social and physical contact among pride members is evident.

PUBLISHED BY THE NATIONAL GEOGRAPHIC SOCIETY
Reg Murphy PRESIDENT AND CHIEF EXECUTIVE OFFICER
Gilbert M. Grosvenor CHAIRMAN OF THE BOARD
Nina D. Hoffman SENIOR VICE PRESIDENT, PUBLICATIONS

THE BOOK DIVISION
William R. Gray VICE PRESIDENT AND DIRECTOR
Charles Kogod ASSISTANT DIRECTOR
Barbara A. Payne EDITORIAL DIRECTOR

BOOK PRODUCTION TEAM
Leah Bendavid-Val PROJECT EDITOR
Lisa Lytton-Smith ART DIRECTOR
Deborah Sussman TEXT EDITOR
Rebecca Barns CONSULTING EDITOR AND RESEARCHER
Rusty Smith LEGENDS WRITER
Kevin G. Craig EDITORIAL ASSISTANT
Jenny Song MAP ARTIST

Library of Congress Cataloging-in-Publication Data

Hunting with the moon.
p. cm.
ISBN 0-7922-7020-7
1. Lions—Botswana—Savuti.
I. National Geographic Society (U.S.)
QL737.C23H87 1997
599.757'09883—dc21 97-7593
CIP

HALF-TITLE PAGE: *Within the pride lions are one big, happy family—until a kill is made, and then every mouthful is fiercely contested.*
TITLE PAGE: *Maome and Motsumi were the dominant lionesses of a pride that ruled the Savuti marsh.*
PAGE 18: *Ntchwaidumela, "he who greets with fire."*

The Lions of Savuti

HUNTING WITH THE MOON

TEXT BY DERECK JOUBERT

PHOTOGRAPHS BY BEVERLY JOUBERT

ACKNOWLEDGMENTS

This book sputtered into life after many a false start as we struggled with our perfectionist handicaps, and a few publishers, until it found its natural and rightful home with the National Geographic Society.

Its inspiration was found in the hours of lonely lion work in Savuti, so the area itself must be thanked. All the people who lived and struggled there are the ones who will truly know what it is like and how much we appreciate their help: Lloyd Wilmot for his generosity; June Wilmot for her shared passion for the Savuti lions; and all at Lloyd's Camp in Savuti for years of friendship and hospitality; Heather and Pat Carr-Hartley for their constant support, Heather for running our lives, fully, consistently, and faultlessly . . . better than we could; Pat for keeping us up-to-date with conservation news; Lorna and Willie Gibson, Beverly's parents, for keeping our business liquid, arranging processing at Beith Laboratories, and sending DHL packages around the world. They generally make sure that we can spend as much time as we physically can with the lions.

We send thanks across the ocean to Deborah Sussman for her judicious editing skills and calming, no-nonsense contribution to our story; and Lisa Lytton-Smith, who guided us through two publishers, was our representative in the front ranks of our fight against imagined nightmares of mediocrity, and designed the end product. Jenny Song from Knysna in South Africa, once a Savuti resident, contributed the detailed paintings that illustrate the prides and their territories.

We also thank Maura Mulvihill, Joanne Wheeler, and April Goebel at Image Collection; Marilyn Gibbons; and Mya Laurinaitis for promoting Beverly's photographic career.

At National Geographic, Gil Grosvenor and Tim Kelly offered friendship and professional interest in our work. The staff of National Geographic Television contributed to our lives as filmmakers and nurtured us during long spells of isolation so that instead of feeling lost when arriving in Washington, D.C., we felt the warmth of home and family.

The lions of Savuti belong to no one, but to everyone in Botswana, and we thank the people of this wonderful country that we have imposed ourselves on, both for their wildlife splendors and their tolerance and acceptance.

Without protection, of course, these lions would be the subject of no more books or films, and during this project Lt. General Ian Khama initiated Botswana's anti-poaching effort carried out by the army. We thank him and the president of Botswana, Sir Ketumile Masire, for the support, the words of advice, and interest over the years, and the Director of Wildlife and National Parks and his staff for kind cooperation and permissions over the last 14 years.

A true labor of love, this book represents long years of observation, years spent soaking up the privilege of being allowed to bear witness to some of the greatest moments in natural history. Not for a moment did we take that precious gift for granted.

Lionesses from Motsumi's pride await the night's hunt.

To all the souls that once were and are no longer: lions, elephants, and people . . . friends all; and to Eric.

"We must accept our pain, change what we can . . . and laugh at the rest."
Camille Paglia

Islands of stone jut out of Lake Savuti, a remnant of an ancient lake known as Mababe. Lionesses give birth in the many lairs found among these eight granite hills.

contents

INTRODUCTION

I can't remember exactly how it felt when it all started, or even why it all started. Perhaps it was growing up with parents who were forever packing a vehicle and heading off to the national parks of South Africa, or having a brother who from the age of six could draw and paint animals as deftly as any art school graduate. Much of my adolescence was spent waiting for my brother, Keith, to return from the wilds of Angola, Zambia, Mozambique, or Botswana; I would listen to his stories while I watched him pack for his next trip.

We were an exploring family. When it came time for me to attend university, I was already biased toward the kind of learning that takes place in wide open spaces. I felt trapped in the 20-by-20-foot university apartment with one small window overlooking the drunks' favorite alley.

After three years, I sprang away from my dingy apartment. On the way, I grabbed the hand of the young woman I loved, the only person in the world who understood what I wanted to be and shared my frustration with the mundane. Beverly Gibson and I had met in high school; her family, like mine, had a history of craving wilderness. As children, she and her twin brother spent enough time chasing each other with spiders that there is still a tomboyish quality to Beverly's beauty.

Armed with enthusiasm, some books by Sir Richard Burton, George Adamson, and great lion scientists like Guttisberg and Schaller, we began our bush careers. For three years we ran game lodges and worked at researching and game ranging. At a lodge called Mala Mala, in South Africa, we encountered the fantastic variety of wildlife that animal behaviorists need to hone their skills. I began to focus on lions. I was intrigued by the differences between the behavior of the lions we observed and what I knew about the behavior of East African lions.

Beverly and I hungered for more time with the lions and more time with each other. And then one day, on a short trip to the Okavango Delta in Botswana, we discovered real wilderness, that slightly scary quality a place has when you realize you could get lost there with very little hope of rescue. By chance we crossed paths with people from the Lion Research Center in Chobe, and within a year we were residents of Savuti, filming our much-loved subjects. It was the beginning of a dream.

We knew that lions lived out most of their lives at night, and we intended to research their nocturnal behavior and capture it on film. We also knew that even if we succeeded, many people would be enraged by the level of interference that they thought our efforts would require. Nevertheless, we unlocked the door and stepped out into the darkness.

Twenty-three thousand hours of lion observation later, after witnessing 5,000 hunting attempts and nearly 1,500 kills, we stepped back in from the experience. Weather-beaten, tired, and 13 years older, we were ready to present ourselves and face our opponents, who turned out to be fewer in number than we had thought. We brought with us a package that contained a world of strangeness.

Looking back, I sometimes feel that I grew up with the lions, and in many ways I have. When we came to the bush to work I was 21, Beverly only 20. We have spent more time with lions than with our parents. We certainly knew we had taken on some of the lions' character when someone called me "Radetau" one day, and the name stuck. In Setswana it means "father of lions."

It may seem strange, but it never occurred to us to fear our subjects. I had experiences with lions that now seem absolutely reckless. And even some of our recent encounters have been hair-raising. One cold night in particular, we were driving toward the camp when we saw a marsh owl in the road. It had caught a mouse, an ideal photo opportunity for Beverly. Dressed in a thick sheepskin jacket and wearing knee-high sheepskin boots, she got out of the vehicle and crawled carefully forward. She heard a movement in the grass beside her and asked me what it was. A flick of the spotlight told me it was zebras, off about 60 yards to the left.

Beverly got a shot, then moved in closer. When she was well ahead of me and the vehicle, she asked about the noise again. I checked; the zebras were about 30 yards away. The owl flew off, Beverly said "thank you" softly under her breath, and I drove up to her. Suddenly the zebras ran. Desperate calls and a blood-curdling yell sounded from behind us. In the lights, just 30 feet back, we saw eight lions on a zebra stallion, right in the road on top of Beverly's tracks. We watched as a young male clamped his jaws firmly on the zebra's throat.

Based on the tracks, we later worked out that the rustling in the grass next to Beverly had been the lions. Fortunately, they were stalking zebras that night and not sheep.

We worked dark nights in a remote area, so it is not surprising that we endured some hardships. We've had to salvage our equipment from lions who were determined to run off with an unattended camera and tripod, resulting in a game of tug-of-war between me and a lioness. Once, while reversing very slowly in a badly potholed section of the marsh, I drove into a six-foot-deep hole hidden in the grass. Beverly was tossed backward from the roof of the truck, head over heels and down through the roof hatch, banging her head so badly that she recovered herself by

Young Tau developed a special bond with the males, who rarely display much tolerance to cubs.

shaking her head repeatedly and looking about as if watching invisible yellow canaries flying in circles around her head. When hyenas made off with her sheepskin jacket, she jumped out and furiously reclaimed it from the startled animals. Shoes, too, have been snatched and then reclaimed. Every week Beverly endured things that other people would consider too much in a lifetime.

It might seem boring, spending all your time watching animals that are active for less than 20 percent of their lives, but as we sat with them during the day, we used the time to write our notes and catch up on research material. When the light faded we were alone with the lions, who quite often slept on into the night.

It was only then that we allowed ourselves to indulge in the peacefulness of reflection, lying on our backs, looking up at the night sky. For hours we talked about what could be out there, the chances of there being another place like this with lions and hyenas and human observers in an identical accident of evolution. On those cold nights, we had time to learn the stars and make up our own shapes in the sky, all while we shared our space on this earth with the lions.

For us there was nothing more comforting than stretching out for a light sleep in the back of our vehicle with the soft, deep breathing of lions all around us, punctuated by the occasional snore or the sound of grass rustling as one of them turned over. Our trust—and theirs—was so great that we could slip into sleep in a vehicle that had no doors and no roof.

Dust clouds rising over northern Botswana trace the meanderings of the buffalo herds.

THE BEGINNING

Savuti breathes. I've never known any place like it. During the hot, dry days of October, it draws in a deep, hollow breath that sucks the moisture from all living things, plants and animals alike. Trees all but crumble to dust, turning white with the effort to survive. Impalas boldly face the breath, but their bodies shrivel and their bones press against their taut skins like the stays of a canoe. People start bickering, and everyone shows signs of wear.

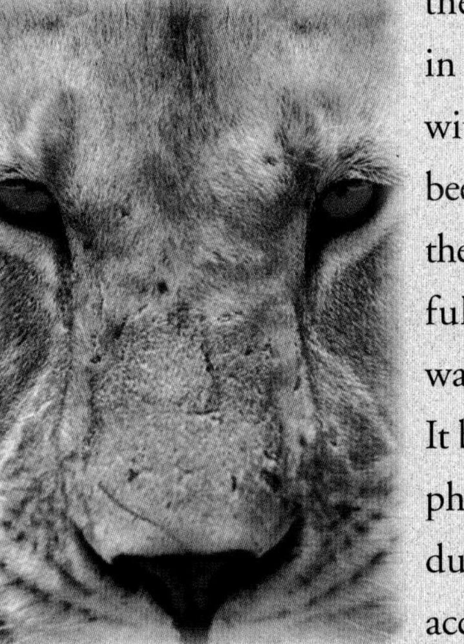

Then, just as the last remaining elephants sway unsteadily on their feet, passing haggard trunks over the wind-parched bones of their fallen companions, the inhaling stops. Everything stills. The wind dies. The heat creeps up a notch or two. It is quiet—for a moment. Then the exhaling begins. First the little breaths, almost as if Savuti doesn't want to release its cruel grip but can't hold on any longer. A different wind stirs in small eddies.

And then the whole of Savuti blows out like an awakening giant. The rains pelt the animals and soak the trees. The people run for cover from the rain they prayed for, and soon begin to curse it as well. It usually happens at sunset, so the double impact of rain and the end of the day punches you in the head, making you dizzy with relief. Impalas and wildebeests have new life pumped into them, and they dance, one gracefully, the other with an awkwardness that is a kind of grace. It blows out so hard that the elephants float away and the white dust turns to mud. Months of accumulated elephant urine and the blood of countless victims are released from the transformed soil and blend with the scent of freshly washed wild sage; the air smells spicy and sweet.

During those explosive months, the sucking in begins again, imperceptibly at first. You realize it only after it has been happening for several weeks. Then it is too late to appreciate what has passed.

It was a hot September day when we first flew into Savuti. We could smell the spicy sage three or four hundred feet above the airstrip. From the plane we saw the wet bodies of herds of elephants, shiny as tiny gray beads scattered in the grass and marshland. The wonderland beneath us looked as secure and long lasting as the mountains of granite that jutted out of the flat landscape like ancient fortresses in a desert.

What we saw from the air and, finally, on the ground was an abundance of animals unlike any we had experienced before. Both Beverly and I had grown up in Africa, and by this time we had worked in the bush for five years, constantly tramping in the dust or bush of any number of wilderness areas, always looking for the ultimate. Now it seemed we had found it. Herds of sable antelopes in numbers we had only read about in accounts by old hunters, elephant bulls so unaffected by our presence that they allowed us to zoom right by in a noisy vehicle without even ceasing their gentle feeding. Giraffes, kudu, impalas, roan antelopes, and, strangest of all to us, the tsessebe herds. We had never seen these in the wild before.

We had come to the Okavango on a holiday and loved the freedom and vastness of the wilderness. Savuti was our next stop; we'd been invited by the Lion Research camp because of our own research work. (We had been working with lions in South Africa in the late 1970s—in fact, Beverly and I had worked almost exclusively with lions from the moment we walked into the bush.) Although we hadn't "discovered" anything new about lions prior to arriving in Botswana, we could see that this was the ideal place to do so. At only 200 square miles, Savuti is small, but it is part of the 4,080-square-mile Chobe National Park, and so it exists as a feature of that larger park, not an isolated "nature island." After a week at Savuti, Beverly and I were determined to move there immediately. Within two weeks of beginning our work with lions in Savuti, we had identified 120 lions, watched them hunting and fighting, mating and with cubs. We fell in love with the area, a love affair that developed into marriage and lifelong dedication.

Savuti, this strange paradise we had chosen as home, relied on the water of the Savuti channel for its survival. When the water started disappearing, we became witnesses to the most heartrending suffering and hardship. Death greeted us around each corner every day. Animals perished, but not before suffering starvation or dehydration.

Even now the reason for that dry-up is still unclear. The beautiful channel of crystal-clear water simply began to change. Almost daily after our arrival the level dropped. Water-level watching is a national pastime in Botswana, but to us, at least at first, it seemed amazing and quite ridiculous. We thought things like mountains and rivers remained constant!

The next two years drastically altered our concept of what is permanent in the world around us. Most surprising was the fact that although we live in a time when news of man's destructive influence on the environment is so common, this event was apparently uninfluenced by humans. The channel had flowed since 1958, with only brief low-water periods in the mid-sixties. Now, in 1982, the water was definitely disappearing.

At first the hippos bunched up into the deepest section of the channel, forming a herd of 120 individuals, but soon they had to move

An impala trembles on the verge of flight.

out into the rapidly drying surrounding bush. Many chose the wrong direction, heading east or south to a certain dusty fate. Those that moved northward had an unknown future; those that went west survived. Twenty-six of them stayed, a remnant of the huge herd, stuck in thick mud, baking in the sun, too weary to leave the last hope of moisture. Finally, as predators like hyenas and lions took advantage of their plight, the last of the hippos died or tried to leave. Conditions had worsened, and the mud engulfed their bodies so completely that movement was difficult. Some had lost so much energy that they simply perished where they were.

Hyenas gathered to feed. The only route to the carcasses was over the backs of the living, but hyenas are brazen, and the surrounding hippos, who had to be content with their own survival, became platforms in the mud. Lions chased around after any hippos that decided it was time to venture out. As each animal left the mud, the gap left was filled by those that remained. No wanderer could ever work his way back into the sludge.

It was an incredible time. Not only were the animals dying around us, but it felt as though the very soul of this place was withering away—and yet we found ourselves appreciating the privilege of being in the right place at the right time, like voyeurs at a scene of an accident. As the river was stolen from the landscape day by day by the hot breeze, the place dried into a dust bowl. It was to keep track of this bizarre process that Beverly picked up a camera and started working seri-

Hippos crowd into what little remains of the shrinking Savuti River channel.

In times of drought, the Savuti water holes provide little more than mud for hundreds of thirsty elephants crowded into the small space.

ously on a record of events. Our desire to document the change also prompted us to begin filming what we were witnessing. Because we were still new to the business of filming, we blundered through the process, relying on our enthusiasm more than any technical expertise, overwhelmed by the spectacle around us.

We found ourselves rushing around, desperately trying to film every aspect of this overwhelming drought and what it was doing to its victims. Each month, each year, the situation extended into other avenues of horror: the year of the elephants digging, the young hippo that miraculously found its way to an elephant dig and braved all to take up occupancy. Everything ended up in our film *The Stolen River,* which is a chronicle of the dry-up. Within two years the Savuti channel was no more—two unbelievable years during which the wild sage smell was overpowered by the ever-present smell of death. Genets, servals, civets, and honey badgers feasted on the dead fish. Hordes of fish eagles and marabou storks circled the ailing channel, defying all ornithological laws about territoriality.

Elephants began digging desperately for hidden underground water.

At first they started on the marsh, excavating holes with their toenails and trunk tips. Then they turned to the channel. In the now dry riverbed they dug deep holes in the sand. Most digs yielded just a few drops, but two or three struck real water. As time dragged on and the water table sank even lower, one water hole remained. We called it "the seep." Each day the elephants drank what they could and smashed away the ground around the sides and in the ever-deepening bed. Every night the water would gently seep back into the depression. The animals crowded in again each day—buffaloes, impalas, elephants, sable and roan antelopes, lions, hyenas, wild dogs, leopards, kudus, warthogs, giraffes, and one lone hippo, all together in one company, all players on a common stage.

Eventually even the seep was struck by the same malady. Its demise spread more hardship. Among those that relied on the seep was a species that didn't use the water but depended on the presence of the other animals: man. At this point the game rangers and safari operators in Savuti stepped in to resuscitate the water source. With the salvation of the seep and later the installation of a water hole filled from a borehole, the first active management of Savuti was born, an interference that is still much debated and agonized over. What would have happened if the region had been left to dry up, the animals allowed to leave or die themselves? Wilderness would have survived. It was at this point that we had to abandon our posts as observers of nature's apparently more destructive roles. We were left with the overpowering feeling that the changes we were witnessing were as natural as hot and cold weather, wet and dry seasons, or day and night. We decided that we had to add our own voices to the ongoing debate about conservation issues in Botswana.

Our own lives thrive on change. Like us, the surface of Africa stagnates without some form of change. Savuti probably couldn't maintain a huge load of animals indefinitely; the fickle water supply ensures the survival of the region. Unfortunately, we as a species have become so efficient at modifying our own lives and the environment around us to suit our immediate needs that we cannot bear to watch negative change, even change that keeps the savannas healthy. Often our good intentions kill. Savuti itself would not necessarily have perished had humans not intervened. A huge area surrounds it, and the placement of one or two water holes is more a symbol than it is an actual influence on the wilderness.

Now every single day of the dry winter season, bull elephants gather around the water hole. Some days we count more than 70 at a time bunched together, patiently waiting their turn to drink. A very firm hierarchy has developed among them, both bonding them and separating the more dominant from the subordinates. When the seep died, as all natural water holes do, a new, artificial water hole took on all the animal traffic. The bulls simply changed location by a few miles and carried on their dominance games. When the bulls completely smashed the sides of the new water hole and dug it so deep that they could swim in the water, humans chose and created a new venue for them—and so we will go on.

Beverly diligently photographed this whole process. After the first year's work, all her photographs were stolen, and she became disheartened and didn't photograph for a while. And while all of this was going on, we had other work to do.

Besides making *Stolen River*, we were in

Savuti to observe and film lions. Chris McBride started the work in the late seventies; in 1981, Petri Viljoen took over for about three years. Later we worked with Sue Cooper, who then switched her focus to hyenas. Throughout this time, we kept track of the lions and concentrated our efforts on recording long-term effects, things that would be difficult for the scientists to include in their work.

Filming lions can be one of the most exciting and stimulating activities imaginable. It works something within that is primeval, frightening, and disturbingly enjoyable. Watching lions hunting is one of the big prizes for anyone, whether you're an avid naturalist or not. It draws up almost forgotten memories of a time when we feared these cats desperately because they were a real threat to our existence—and knowing your enemy brings you closer to knowing yourself.

Even today, however, it is almost impossible to convince those who live on the edge of civilization in Africa, people who come into periodic contact with perhaps just the sounds of lions, that these are glorious and important creatures. They would much rather look at a dead lion than live with the knowledge that some magnificent animal capable of tearing them to pieces is loose in the wild. I'm convinced that romanticizing the dangerous is a Western luxury. But both Beverly and I are romantics, and we set about our task with a passion.

We were also committed to the goal of convincing people, mainly those who lived with wild Africa as their neighbor, that this continent in its wildest form is good and not an embarrassment to be refashioned after the prosperous West or the moralistic East. The world looks at Africa as the wealthiest continent in wildlife currency. Often Africa shuns its oldest, most valuable asset.

Sixteen hours a day we slogged away, through the cold August nights and wet December days. The worst was when the below-freezing night temperatures butted up against the 110-degree days; our bodies, sandwiched between these opposing forces, felt like exploding. This dramatic variation seems much less so when one has a fire and warm bed to escape to, but we couldn't afford to escape. We wanted to saturate ourselves with as much lion behavior as possible, to be with the lions continuously. Only by doing this could we even remotely hope to discover, and then communicate, exactly what they were doing all the time. We felt frustrated by the lack of information that confronted us: The stories told by hunters from previous generations, and even scientists' studies, could provide us with only scattered information about what lions did at night. Hunters around their campfires were visited by lions only occasionally, and scientists, not wanting to influence lion behavior with lights, went out mainly around the full moon. Our own observations in other areas hinted at a wealth of undiscovered information. It now became our job to investigate and reveal the real lives of lions at night.

Mandevu, ever alert to a range of sensations beyond human perception.

In the long, dry winter between zebra migrations, the wildebeest is an important prey species for the lions.

Hunting during daylight hours is unusual for the lions of Savuti, but the temptation of an easy kill is irresistible.

Although lions are good hunters, they are not averse to scavenging. A huge bull elephant provides a meal that lasts ten days.

THE PRIDE

A single bee flies through space. He lands on a green leaf—a croton bush, bitter to the taste—and flies off again. Now he is low level, out of the blue, skimming the brittle grass tops. Something attracts him. His senses are attuned in this dry time to moisture. Something in the grass has it. He swings around with a buzz of vibrating wings and circles the source, confirming its presence. Then he slows, drops his legs, and lands. That is when the explosion happens. It is so strong that it blows him about a hundred bee-body lengths, soaking him in moisture that covers even his wings. In flight he shakes himself dry and tries again. His brain has got a fix on that moisture now like a geographical positioning system, and he lands again. This time he tastes the moisture. The source is buried inside a hole 20 times his size, which he explores. It moves a little, but the bee is used to operating even in high winds on tiny flowers. In the darkness he follows the rivulet of moisture then, bang! He is exploded out again into the blue nothingness, sprayed with water.

The unfortunate bee had landed on a lion's nose—a very irritating phenomenon for the lion, especially because even as the bee tumbled through the air a second time, it was locking on for a return trip. Worse still was the fact that 200 more of these insects were on their way.

The lions, Tshaba's pride, had had a rough night. They had walked eight miles and killed three impalas, but it was not enough for 17 large lions. They lay in the shade of the mitsibi trees. The persistent bees pestered them to the point of distraction. Sneezes could be heard from every quarter, and each lion shook its head furiously from time to time. They were definitely uncomfortable. One by one they tried to sneak away into the thick cover, but no cover is too thick for a bee.

We filmed all this and watched with amusement—until the bees discovered our canvas water bag, which hung on the side of the vehicle next to Beverly. Soon we had a hundred or more bees inside and around the water bag.

The sun was on its way down under another beautiful winter sky, a huge red ball that would hang suspended for over an hour just above the horizon. The effects of dust particles in the air played color tricks on us.

We decided to move out, away from the spluttering lions, to watch the sunset. The bees followed. We didn't mind, but at sunset they tend to want to go for cover if they're not near their hive. Where we stopped we could see the red ball finally slipping out of the sky. The bees began to swarm, and we watched them all disappear into a hole in the ground right next to Beverly. "That's a handy hole for them," she said. Suddenly a warthog came rocketing out of the hole and raced toward the sun, followed by a pale pink stream of dust.

The lions heard the warthog explosion and reacted with the vigor that is their usual response to such opportunities. In the low light it was difficult to see, but from the pink dust trails we could make out that the warthog was exercising some very delicate maneuvers to escape the lions.

It's true that the high point of lion watching, and the focus of their lives, is killing. But they spend very little of their lives killing things, and once you've seen a number of kills, you can appreciate all the other lion behavior, which is in fact far more rewarding.

The real beauty of lions is in their social behavior. In general, lions' social lives are complex but easy to follow and understand —unlike those of hyenas, which are very difficult to figure out. One of our first tasks was to get to know each and every lion in the pride well enough so that in the middle of a hunt, for example, Beverly could say, "On the left Maome stalking in, right side we have Smudge and Thaka. Front is Motsumi." Individual "mug shots" of the lions were a great way to identify them. Most have some kind of marking, and their whisker patterns are as unique in their own way as elephant ears, zebra stripes, or our own fingerprints. After a while we used the photographs simply as backup information because we had come to know each lion by character and general appearance. Not too surprisingly, the lions also came to know us.

Maome's pride, young and vital when we arrived, proved more individualistic than any we have known. Each lioness's character shone from her so brightly that even at a distance we could recognize them. Maome and her sisters had been forced to split from the group led by Tshaba, their mother. Less than two years old, Maome had been cast out to grow or die, to form a new pride or disappear.

We met her again months later and observed her mating. When she gave birth to cubs, it was an opportunity for us to follow a group of females from their birth until their death (or ours—whichever came first). This was our aim.

One of the cubs seemed to exude a different, more intense kind of energy, an energy that matched Savuti itself. By the age of 2½, she was a full-fledged female member of the pride. She was called Motsumi, meaning "huntress" or "of the hunt" because of her superior hunting prowess. She distinguished herself not only in her hunting but in her appearance, her spirit for conflict (whether with hyenas

Bone-crushing jaws gently grip a cub's delicate neck on long translocations through the bush.

The incessant demands of a four-week-old cub evoke growls of sleepless irritation from its mother.

or with rival prides), and her sheer dignity. One contact with a rival pride left her limping like a labrador with hip disease, her lacerated back swollen for months, but her wounds did nothing to dampen the energy with which she defended her pride.

The life cycle of a lion is fairly straightforward. There are, of course, variations within that; it is the variations that are so intriguing. Cubs go through a number of phases. They are born with their eyes open, but initially they probably can't see too well. Because they are less vulnerable than a lot of other animals, they are not well developed as new cubs and are totally dependent on their mothers for a long time (very much like humans).

Soon they are brought out of isolation and introduced to the other pride members. An important factor governing their survival at this stage is stability of the pride. If a pride is stable, all the females will have developed a synchrony where they come into mating readiness, or estrus, simultaneously; consequently, they are mated and have cubs about the same time. If the synchrony is working, a pride will suddenly have a flood of cubs to contend with. One case in Savuti was typical. Tshaba's pride of ten females all came into estrus at once. Furious mating erupted—for weeks it was all we saw the poor males do. Only two males serviced the ten females, so there was little time for eating, and they all lost weight dramatically. As a result of these many successful matings, 27 cubs were born at roughly the same time.

This sort of synchrony facilitates survival.

A lioness encourages her cub's development of climbing and balancing skills.

If one female dies, her cubs find themselves in a massive "cub-pool" in which all cubs suckle from any mother. They can then survive just as well as the others. In fact, the "cub-pool" system is so effective that it is difficult to tell if individual mothers and their cubs actually recognize one another after a few months.

The cubs then go through at least a year of pure play and communal living. After this, there seems to come a change. Over the next few months they will be fully weaned, and, in addition, their play will take on an educational emphasis. They become active in hunts, and although they often mess up great opportunities, their mistakes are tolerated by the rest of the pride.

Cubs are always fun to watch, a delight we often need, especially after we've been working with adult lions that have been involved in the killing and fighting that make up most of their active lives. Cubs look cute, of course, but it's their behavior that fascinates us. They get to an age when everything is a new experience. At night if they are taken out with the adults, they often break away to check out a hole or movement in the grass, then have to run to catch up.

Cubs are interested in just about everything, but they can't yet distinguish between the safe and the not-so-safe. Very few healthy adults bother with porcupines, and even the sub-adults know better, but cubs have to try. (Very old lions and lions that are desperate tend to disregard all previous knowledge and try once again to kill porcupines. They are seldom successful.) When lions do decide to investigate or play with porcupines, it is a comical sight—if they don't make contact. The porcupine rushes at the lions stamping its feet and rustling its quills, sounding very much like a flamenco dancer. Then the lions have to dive out of the way or be prepared for a painful spike in the body.

Another object of curiosity for cubs is a tortoise. A group of cubs was lying under a spiny gardenia tree when a careless tortoise walked toward the same patch of shade. One young cub approached, not quite stalking but definitely interested. Carefully the miniature lion patted out at the tortoise, which ducked its head and legs into the protective shell. That startled the lion cub, and he stood back to wait for any advance. When there was no more movement, the cub lay down with the shell between his front legs and struggled to get his jaws around the strange new object. After nearly an hour the cub managed to pick the tortoise up, but the weight of the animal was too much and it thudded to the ground upside down. With a last pat of the paw that spun the tortoise around, the lion cub departed for the shade. He flopped down under the tree but kept a keen eye on the upended tortoise still spinning in the sun.

It is the age of investigation and exploration, but this first year of a cub's life is also the most dangerous.

Maome's group was on the eastern road of the marsh, walking casually, not particularly hunting anything, spread out haphazardly. The grass parted to our left and the toughest of all the animals emerged with a grunt. A honey badger! First it charged the vehicle. We stopped, and it ran on ahead toward the lions. One of the cubs saw it coming and turned to ambush it. Its black skin, a shaggy coat with a white stripe down the middle, seemed to be too loose on its body. Puffing like a steam engine it trotted straight into the center of the lion pride, not stopping for anything. The cub ran out to mock attack but stopped dead in its tracks when the honey badger turned to meet him, instantly aggressive. The females saw the cub in trouble and came in, surrounding the badger more by coincidence than design. Even this surprise development didn't faze the honey badger, who spun around at the nearest lion, growling loudly and flashing its teeth. Without stopping it went for each lioness in the circle. The lions bailed out of their circle one by one and ran off a few paces, opening up a path for the little aggressor to continue on its way, which he did with a few more snarls and grunts, breaking branches and twigs noisily in the bushes as he left. The interaction was so disturbing for the lions that they all greeted afterwards and took a rest period for a few hours before moving on again.

Female lions spend every day of their lives with each other, with few separations in a lifetime of about 12 years. Sisters must know each other better than we can begin to imagine. Sisters born to the same mother suckle from the same milk supply, share each meal, mate with the same males, even share the same cubs (if the synchrony is working), and fight the same battles for a dozen years.

The familiarity is obvious when you see a pride at play. When the sun begins to set, the

The pride swells as new mothers bring their cubs down from lairs in the hills.

Cubs left alone usually cower together until called, but there are always those natural-born mischief-makers who invariably end up in trouble.

Savuti lions get up to start the night's activities. While they stretch and yawn and get ready to go, one lioness might drop her head into a mischievous semi-stalking posture, trot up behind the next lioness, and jump up onto her back. A short growl and they separate, and the games begin. The leader drops down into the grass, turning to ambush one of the unsuspecting walkers.

She leaps out just ahead of the others, not too late to make contact but leaving enough warning space to allow the attacked to sprint away—after all, what is a game without a chase? As she pursues her "victim," the chaser often becomes the chased, either when a third female joins the game or when the escaping lioness turns the tables on her attacker.

At the end of the run, the pursued, if caught, will flop down in mock capture, rolling over and patting out at the other lionesses, biting softly. We have never seen a claw unsheathed in these games, although there is roughness, and on occasion a lion does get slightly hurt. This is followed by a short growl and a moment of seriousness before she herself initiates another game. Sometimes the whole pride will chase one lioness, and the lot collapses in a heap of soft bodies.

In an anthropomorphic mood, you can see a real sense of mischief in lions. Maome's pride, for example, was a group of lions who truly seemed to enjoy themselves and each other. As far as we could tell, the play that these adults engaged in served no purpose other than to increase or secure a bond—or perhaps simply to provide entertainment.

Tau bolted from cover to cover, his agility and small size keeping him undetected and alive.

As much as we both hate to be accused of anthropomorphism, we believe that animals have emotions, and our proof of that has developed over years of studying lions.

We came across Tau, a little lion of just three months, wandering aimlessly on the edge of the marsh, which was a prime hyena area. He'd become separated from his pride. It was the time of the zebra migration through Savuti, and zebra contact calls could be heard everywhere. By nightfall the little lion was exhausted. We had kept our distance in order not to chase him or increase his stress level, and twice we had to duck away behind some bushes because tourists came by. We believe lions are to be shared, and under normal circumstances we would not have hidden, but we knew that the people would inadvertently have confused the little lion cub and ruined any chance for his survival.

That night, he climbed a low tree and huddled up in a fork, shivering against the cold. Bundled in our thick sweaters and warm jackets, we felt more than a pang of guilt. It was miserably cold. We took shifts watching him, but we might as well just have slept, because by dawn he hadn't moved, except to look up at any passing creature or hint of activity. When the light came, the lion cub climbed down and walked about half a mile. A tourist vehicle raced by, but he ducked into the shade of a croton bush next to the road and waited out the rest of the day there. Then he wandered south, even farther from his mother's territory, and night fell again.

When some hyenas passed by, the cub

bolted up a very convenient tree. The hyenas smelled around the base of the tree and left. Then, out of the dark, a much lighter, larger shape appeared—a lioness. The little lion ran down the tree and raced to meet her. She saw him coming, stopped, and lay down. We didn't recognize this lioness. Later, through a close search of records, we discovered that she was a nomadic female who only periodically used this area. But the cub didn't know that. With tail held high and head up he ran to greet her, prepared for the head-rubbing greeting ritual that even at his age he'd already learned well. The lioness growled fiercely. The cub answered with a guttural meow, but still the female rejected him. He stopped short and meowed again, then circled behind her, trying to close the distance by approaching from behind. The lioness growled again and stood up. The cub rolled over submissively, and the lioness turned and walked away in the direction from which she'd just come.

The little lion got up and called, and called again, then ran down the path after her. He could never have caught up, and, within minutes, he was lost again, away from the treeline—out in the marsh. He sat down on his rear end, front legs still planted, and looked out into the darkness that had swallowed the lioness. He was a forlorn sight.

By now we were feeling a little better about our non-interference policy, but not much.

As we waited with the lion cub, some zebras panicked. They began calling and stampeding, not far ahead of us but out of sight in the moonless night. Within minutes we could hear the culmination of the hunt: a zebra foal's cries were drowned out by the confused babble of hyenas' calls. The young lion cub took fright at the sound of hyenas and dashed into the grass on the right. In a flash we had lost him, only to discover a pair of eyes on top of a large termite mound sticking out of the grass. From this vantage point he looked out at the hyenas as they finished off their kill.

For five days we stayed with the cub as he found his way back to the trees and cover and spent a few more miserable nights, one of which torrented down with rain. By now he was no doubt low on his reserves, and the rain probably didn't help. He looked tired and close to the point of collapse.

Dawn of the fifth day was cold, with a lot of dew after the rain. Zebras spread out across the marsh, golden in the first rays of backlight. Again the little lion lay draped helplessly over an anthill, trying to keep out of the wet grass thawing in the morning marsh. Suddenly his ears swivelled around, pointing forward, and we heard the first cough that sets off a lion roar. It was a roar we knew well: the pride male.

The little lion jumped down from his perch into the sodden grass and ran toward the roars. We followed at a distance. Following was easy, as the cub left a path in the dew, and ahead we could see the long grass parting and closing behind him as he ran.

It was over a mile, but he didn't stop once. When we saw the pride lying in the open we circled around the incoming cub and set up cameras in anticipation.

The pride was all present. As the grass

Lions bond socially by playing together.

parted and the lion cub emerged, one lioness jumped up to investigate. The cub meowed and heads turned. He greeted the female but wasted no time in getting to each member of the pride, even disobeying decorum and leaping up onto the male's back as he lay sprawled in the dewy grass. The surprised male jerked his head up but didn't growl at the cub, who by then had tumbled off into the grass on his way to another lion. For once we had witnessed a true success story in the bush, and a good lesson to us that by interfering we could have caused more damage than good. At best we could have taken the abandoned cub to some sort of human care situation. Usually it's a zoo or game park. A life back with his pride by far outweighs that. Our resolve never to interfere, especially for whimsical sentiments, was strengthened.

Shortly after his return to the pride we noticed the slightly older cubs playing roughly with the young male. Sometimes a rough play session like this is stopped by the lioness, but this one continued. As the cubs played, the young male tried to escape, but with much shorter strides he was quickly overtaken and caught, often by the tail. So frequent was this rough play and so often was his tail used as an anchor that we filmed him being used like a wheelbarrow every day for a week. Eventually the tip of his tail came off completely, chewed by his older cousins. But a character like this doesn't fade away, and he stayed around for some time with the pride.

After the cubs' second year, their mothers may come into estrus again, and, for the growing cubs, the trouble begins. Their fathers are mating with their mothers, and, if during the last two years a female has died, it is possible that their sisters are being mated. They approach hesitantly whenever the pride gathers because they are wary of the males. The males occasionally lash out if a young male approaches them or gets too close to a female. This tense behavior is difficult for the females to live with, and so the situation worsens. Usually, because lions look so similar, they use scent and sometimes visual clues, like confident behavior, to acknowledge known pride members. Now the young males act strangely, and even the females growl and chase them. The time is drawing nearer for a total break; that time comes after the arrival of new cubs, if not before. The older cubs' mothers can no longer tolerate them and they must go. Armed only with a year's good hunting education, they become nomads, fending for themselves. At this point sometimes sisters follow the young males. In many ways this is a handicap, because although females are better at hunting than young males, they, like their mothers, will come into estrus, and that means trouble for any associated young male.

Wherever they go, these young females drop their sexual scents, which attract adult males. Adult males dominate, mating with the females and chasing the young males.

This nomadic phase is typified by three-year-old males in small groups. They have become expert at nothing but avoiding trouble. They seldom roar, and they keep a very low profile. They scavenge from hyenas, but if hyenas start to retaliate with a seriously vocal counterattack, they leave quickly in case the commotion attracts the resident male lions. They wander ceaselessly. Seldom have identified sub-adults been seen again in the original area. What we can gather is that they find a place some years later, like the incoming nomads that arrive in Savuti from other places. By that time, they are five years old. Their manes are not good, but they no longer resemble punk rockers or Mohicans. Their roars are young and forced, but they are challengers. Something has told them to stay and fight this time, not to run as usual. If they are to stand a chance at all, they must outnumber the territorial males. A good ratio is three or four five-year-olds to challenge two seven-year-old territorial males. The older the old lions are, the better for the challengers, but ultimately territory owners always have something

When darkness falls, the world of the Savuti marsh belongs to Mandevu.

As males get older they become even less tolerant of cubs.

special going for them, like the ancient warriors of Homer's *Iliad* who had invisible gods protecting them.

Sometimes it takes a fight, sometimes the old males know they are beaten. An old pride male we called Duma heard the newcomers and quietly led his females away into the mopane. It was a sure sign of the end. Because the females attract the new males with their estrus scents, contact is inevitable. We never saw Duma again, but within a month the females were flirting with the new young males, who had become firmly entrenched in Duma's old territory.

In the north, three of the most beautiful lions we've ever seen ruled one territory. Tourists named the magnificent males a confusing variety of names, but to us these three "lions of darkness" were known as Tona, Tsididi, and Nyatsi. Tona, the largest of the three, had thick, long, dark mane hair that so engulfed his head, shoulders, back, and the underside of his belly that he looked clumsy when he walked. Apart from their behavior during mating, the three males were extremely close.

During their reign, Tona, Tsididi, and Nyatsi paraded about like three great kings sharing their domain. No intruder was tolerated. All old males were expelled, and all cubs of the old were killed. But together these stern kings were like tender young cubs, greeting each other constantly, rubbing their giant heads together, rolling over together and displaying a companionship I have never seen before or after. In the half moonlight we used to drive alongside the three males as they marched

Territories are contested and defended by males and females.
Spectacular territorial battles between females from different prides often result in fatalities.

abreast on patrol. We could see them without using our lights and often, to stretch our own weary limbs, we would set the vehicle in low-range four-wheel drive, allowing it to chug along unaided, and walk next to it for an hour or more. On these occasions we would find ourselves beside the three males, all of us walking abreast. We were amazed by their tolerance of us, as well as by their beauty and their noble air. There is something uniquely awe-inspiring about a male lion in his prime.

New males have reached their prime when they have a pride of females, with their cubs, and possibly a second pride as well. If the timing of all this goes wrong, if one female goes out of synchrony, there is an unfortunate domino effect. She has cubs before all the others do. Her cubs, because they require too much energy, may die or be abandoned. Even if they do survive to become older cubs, their mother will be in estrus again one year before the other females. She may be mated again and have cubs, but then by the time the other females' cubs are ready to leave the pride, our single female still has very young cubs.

Each new wave of estrus may attract new males. Average tenure by a pride male lion is two to three years. If the new males win their challenge and take over the pride, then the females have problems. Their cubs will be hunted down and killed, primarily because the main ecological function of male lions is to propagate their own genes. This infanticide has the effect of clearing away old "tired" genes and bringing the females into estrus again. (If females lose cubs, they can come

On the marsh there is no escape from the elements.

into estrus again almost immediately. We saw Motsumi mating again just 19 days after she had lost her cubs.)

Two years of stability will go by. The system enforces synchrony by limiting the survival of those born outside it. And then, one day, the pride will hear new males roaring in the distance, and the choice will present itself again to the older males: defend or abdicate.

The females have a slightly more linear life. They experience the same pattern of events that their male siblings do, until the nomadic phase. Then, if the pride needs to recruit numbers to keep a general female population static, the young females will stay with their mothers and will be secure there as pride members until they die. If the pride is at capacity, they will go with their siblings for a while until they are claimed by some resident male along the way.

After the big male takeover of territory, ousted males may have another shot at a takeover of their own, unless they are older than nine or ten years. Then their lives return to nomadic wandering. Seldom are they seen again, although in two cases we did see old males come back to their areas.

In the winter of 1984, a lion called Lyall came back to Savuti. He had been darted and collared long before we moved to Savuti and was definitely ousted before 1979. When he returned, Petri Viljoen darted him to remove the collar, releasing the old lion from his burden. That night we examined the drugged animal. His feet were incredibly worn, his pads chipped and crossed with long, deep cracks. It looked like old Lyall had made a long, hard journey to get back to Savuti.

A second incident was almost identical. In the early eighties, two males, Sequela and Moroko, dominated the south. When three new males arrived, these two males were ousted.

In 1984 Sequela arrived back, very much worse for the wear. Moroko, we were convinced, had already died.

Sequela moved through the northern area, far from his old territory, eating what he could. An old rotten hyena made up one meal, a porcupine another. At a scavenged buffalo kill, hyenas attacked and bit his tail. His resistance and immune system were so low that the tail began to rot. Although he ate a great deal of the buffalo, he didn't put on weight, and he was too tired to move into the shade and away from the vultures. A hooded vulture landed near the carcass and pecked away at anything that looked good to eat, including old Sequela's tail, which came off surprisingly easily.

Without a tail, and with a mane that bunched into clumps like islands in a sea of bare skin, he looked a pitiful sight. Of course, the cry went out to shoot the lion before he became a man-eater. Fortunately, he disappeared that same day. The next night we were 18 miles south, in his old territory with his old pride, when suddenly all the lionesses changed direction and started walking eagerly to the west. We thought they must have heard buffalo. Then they all stopped. From the darkness came the tragic figure of Sequela, the lion equivalent of King Lear.

Continually the lionesses greeted him, and although the new pride males did not, strangely enough they did not attack him either.

All hunting stopped for the night as the lions gathered around, smelling and rubbing heads with their old pride male. By sunrise they were all still around our vehicle, including Sequela.

A game department vehicle drove up, and immediately we thought the worst: "They have come to shoot Sequela." But it was just the regional warden, our old friend John Ben, who happened to be driving by. After we had discussed where he had been and what we had seen, he looked at the lions all around us and said, "Shame. Look at that old man. He will be dead before I reach the Mababe gate." (The Mababe gate was at the southern boundary of the park.) "But he needs the dignity of his own death."

John drove off, and the pride started moving to shade. As I filmed, the old male got up to follow, greeted one female with a gentle head touch, and walked toward the shade. A gentle breeze that barely stroked the grass made him falter in his stride, and he lost balance and toppled over. From where we sat we could look into his yellow eyes and see that there was no life in them. It was 10:29 a.m.; John Ben probably reached the south gate around noon. Over the next two nights hyenas ate Sequela, just as he had eaten one of them a few weeks before.

Did he come back to his old territory for a reason? Was it simply out of desperation for food that he was hoping to scavenge from his old pride? Surely he must have been aware of the risks. Some would even say he came to say goodbye.

Adventurous cubs often strike out on their own to explore the neighborhood. The ability to climb trees can save them from marauding hyenas and other perils.

Interlopers are immediately surrounded and attacked. This young nomadic male will have to look elsewhere to establish himself.

AFTER DARK

It is nearly midnight. The lions lie out in the marsh, dotting the ground like small, dark anthills. At first, it looks as if the moonlight has spread a blue wash over everything; the only indication of the lions' presence is the periodic disappearance of an anthill into the faintly paler blue tapestry in front of us. Gradually, I begin to see other colors as well, and can distinguish details.

A lioness glides silently past the vehicle, her head held lower than the shoulders that seem to work mechanically under her supple skin. She pauses next to us, only five yards from my leg, and looks not at me but over her left shoulder toward something else, something silent and invisible to us. She retraces her steps, coming back toward us, and then slips away into a wide arc until we can only calculate roughly where she was in the gloom. From time to time we can pick out her flat shape through the night glasses, but other objects begin their stealthy maneuvering at the same time.

After an hour they have moved 55 yards. The right flank is more than 200 yards from us, and on the left, at 300 yards or more, the hint of a dark head marks the other edge of the killing field. This is a deadly game.

The moon is in its last quarter. Within minutes total darkness will deny us our already feeble vision. Suddenly, just as the moon begins to turn orange, a loud explosion of wind bursts from the mouth of a prospective victim. "Anthills" loom up in the darkness, and the gates on the killing field close shut as the lionesses appear from everywhere. Beverly flicks the light switch and real color fills our eyes momentarily. A zebra on the run, heading straight for the flank lioness on the right. Two female lions bound along behind the zebra, gaining ground slowly. The flank is nowhere to be seen. Three lionesses charge in from the side, bringing the count to five, but the chase is too much for one lioness near the tail and she drops out. By now they have covered 300 yards in a curve, and still four lionesses tail the frantic zebra. We watch them through the image intensifier, a night-sight that allows us to observe the lions by moonlight only. The lioness closest to the prey finds herself within a good leap of the flying hooves, but the action is too fast.

In the grass the lone lioness can't possibly see any of this. She must rely on other senses to tell her that out there the trap has been sprung and her companions are taking up the chase . . . right toward her. She waits and must hear, as we do, the wheezing of the zebra as its lungs strain to fill and empty as fast as they can, pumping oxygen into the blood stream, pushing energy into those burning muscles. Suddenly the tall grass above her bursts open, the racing zebra with its flaying hooves almost upon her. Like a spring loaded to respond on this cue she is up in a split second with both front legs spread and her claws unsheathed.

The collision sounds like a train shunting. Stationary lioness and speeding zebra become one for an instant. The lioness takes the full force of the impact in the chest and slams to the ground, with the zebra on top of her. As the chasing lionesses' momentum carries them into the struggle, the dust rises lazily, curtaining the horror of the kill.

This was our nightly spectacle for years. While this excitement was going on, we were scrambling around fixing lights in position, aiming, focusing and setting light readings, adjusting the sound recorder, and, on a good night, actually triggering the cameras while getting the vehicle in close enough to film but not so close as to be a major distraction or influence.

Sometimes we got it. More often by far we didn't. Sometimes the lions missed the kill. (Perhaps the waiting lioness was in the wrong position altogether and only lifted her head out of the grass when the noise of the chase subsided in the distance.) Other times the chase and kill were executed perfectly, but behind the vehicle or out of range of the lenses and lights.

For the tense and highly strung this sort of work is not recommended. In the beginning, when we were filming for the Lion Research station and the production planning was non-existent or at best haphazard, we should have had no pressure, but we created our own. Missing so much was very frustrating. Slowly we designed systems that were easy to set up, until we knew that if we did our job perfectly and we still missed the action, then at least we could not blame ourselves. By the time we worked on *Eternal Enemies*, our own production on lions and hyenas, we were very calm about missed opportunities and very philosophical about enjoying the moment.

Each night, as the lions began their evening activities, we would follow roughly one hundred yards behind. If it was Maome's pride, they usually began by running and playing energetically, jumping up on each others' backs, rolling over or stalking and mock-attacking one another. Then, as if some silent signal had been passed among them, play ceased, and they would start walking in earnest, following whoever chose to lead the way. (Leaders appear to be random, as does the direction they choose for the evening. Many times we have sat the whole day observing lions as they watched a steady stream of buffalo or zebra file out of the mopane forest, only to have to follow the lions in exactly the opposite direction after dark. They often baffle us

The pride stares into the night, listening beyond the darkness.

totally—which is no doubt why we still enjoy working with them so much.)

When the lions set off as a group to hunt, we closed the gap between us and them, almost becoming one of the pride. Maome's group spent more than 80 percent of its time on the fringe or in the grassland of the Savuti marsh, parts of which are ideal for following lions with a vehicle. By 1984, we had an improved version of a camera vehicle, a Toyota Land Cruiser that was totally remodeled to accommodate all our camera equipment and the lighting batteries and equipment, as well as our bedrolls and food. In some terrain we were able to move in as close as ten yards at times, without disturbing the pride.

We never maintained this distance for too long before dropping back or switching the engine off.

At the slightest sign that the lions wanted to stop and listen, we would stop. Our vehicle was specially designed to be silent and rattle-free, with rubber coating throughout. Getting close helped us break down whatever resistance the pride may have built up during the day and helped them feel confident that it was us again, and not someone else. We developed a regular ritual of approach that they came to associate with us.

Often at night we would drive among Maome's pride as if we were part of the group, just another lion bringing up the rear. At times, if the males were along for the night, lagging behind or lying down to rest while the females moved on, we would pass them and continue with the females. On these occasions we were truly among the lions, because if the females moved too far ahead the males would bring up the rear, behind us.

In the dull light the sight of the males walking side by side was awesome, sparking comparisons to warriors or gallant knights: the most regal of animals, marching shoulder to shoulder, ready to take on whatever the night could offer.

Each evening by the hour our distance from the lions changed according to what they were doing. We were tensely aware of each body posture, every turned ear or tail movement that could signal that we were too close, or that they had heard something or sensed prey.

Sometimes they chose the distance. One night when the moon was up and the pride slept heavily, we bedded down in the back of the vehicle for some rest of our own. As usual we were within ten yards of most of the lions so we could wake when they roused themselves and greeted each other gently with the soft moans of communication that are typical of their close-bonded social group. One lioness was away, but all the others were present.

Just after 2:00 a.m. we were awakened by a heavy thud against the vehicle. We had overslept slightly, and we could see as we looked over the side the whole pride actively chasing around the vehicle, playing a game of tag in the moonlight. In their excitement and speed they bumped against the vehicle now and then. Their acceptance of us was obvious when Motsumi, the lioness who'd been missing earlier, raced away from a sister and leapt up onto the front of the car, and then off again.

She had gone missing for one day, and

Male lions reputedly scavenge from females but, in Savuti, males participate in the kills.

this night we could see why. In her absence she had lost a few pounds in weight, and the telltale marks of dried blood on her back legs were obvious clues to her condition. When she slowed down and the excitement subsided, giving the pride an opportunity to give her whole body a thorough sniffing over, we could also see her recently suckled nipples.

The next morning just after sunrise, she left the pride again without a parting ritual of any kind and headed south. We expected to be sent off with a growl, or at least given the slip on a long and devious route, but Motsumi was totally trusting. She walked nearly five miles south to an island in the marsh, with us in tow, straight to her young cubs.

Every two or three nights after that Motsumi would leave the cubs and track down the pride. It was always heartwarming to witness the greetings she was given and the excitement her arrival caused, but she had little time for formalities and each time she would trot away from the social activities and lead the others out to hunt.

As I mentioned earlier, Motsumi means "huntress" in Setswana, and that was her calling. Within a few minutes of her arrival the whole of the pride was up and actively hunting. On her second return after having the cubs, Motsumi ran in and greeted everyone, but before they could all gather and settle, she trotted away northward. They followed, and she slowed to let them catch up. Ahead zebras were filing out of the capassa grove into the grassland. When she heard them, the new mother started running again.

Usually a zebra hunt involves a lengthy stalking approach, slow and seemingly well calculated, with two or more flanking lionesses and some attackers creeping in for a direct approach.

Motsumi had no time for this. She conducted herself as if she was charging in for a buffalo hunt or even a lion fight. The other lions stopped and watched. One lowered her head and backed away to circle, but she was too late—caution was already in the wind. Motsumi ran straight into the line of zebras, and before they saw her she was among them. Her full weight knocked down an adult mare. The herd scattered but the stallion mustered his kinship group for a rescue attempt, and like circus horses they turned back in a circle and ran at the lioness. Motsumi did not even release her stranglehold as they ran over her, chopping with their hooves, kicking out at her with their back legs. Somehow she seemed to get smaller, melting into the grass and shielding herself behind the downed zebra, still hanging on to her prize.

The rest of the pride moved in, running as much for the rescuers as for the spoils of the kill. From out of the darkness one of the males launched his attack on the fleeing zebra family, and in a stroke another adult mare disappeared into the grass, a bundle of out-of-control stripes covered by tawny shapes.

Motsumi was as fearsome on her kill as the male usually is on his, not allowing too many of the females to feed. Usually the lioness who actually makes first contact rarely gets to feed on the best meat. Often she is so busy killing that the others arrive and choose their positions before she can release the stranglehold.

The transition from friendly cooperation during a hunt to ferocious competition once the kill has been made is an unforgettable, Jekyll and Hyde characteristic of lion behavior.

Every scrap of meat counts, and none of it comes easily for subadults in their nomadic phase.

Motsumi's kill was completed swiftly, and she commanded the carcass. After an hour she looked up with a bloodied face at the waiting lionesses and stepped away. Immediately they rushed in to take over the rest of the zebra as Motsumi disappeared into the darkness again to find her way back to her cubs.

Before her cubs were introduced to the pride, at roughly five weeks, Motsumi led the lionesses in ten hunts, which accounted for almost all of what they caught in that time.

The more hours we spent following the lions, the more our lives began to adapt to this new strange schedule of living at night and sleeping during the day. Every night was more or less the same: Out by 4:00 each afternoon, find the pride before they start waking up, follow them until something happens or we collapse from exhaustion. Some nights were easier than others, but I remember all too vividly many nights of following behind Maome's pride as the sun came up again. We would work with them while the light was really good in the morning and then follow until the heat got to them. Only then would we either return to camp or steal away to sleep in the shade. By 4:00 p.m. we were back with them.

Minimizing the interference caused by our presence at night was a constant task. We investigated all methods: image-intensifying night-viewing electronic devices, red filtered lights, blue filtered lights, no lights, driving to the side of the lions, lagging behind until they killed something. Ultimately, we found that this last option works best.

Lions can go for long periods without water, surviving on that in the blood of their prey. If water is available, however, they will drink many times a day.

7:30 p.m. Lions get up, stretch, and walk from their shade tree into the marsh to begin hunting. They were stimulated by the hyenas that tested a herd of zebras and set them running.

8:11 p.m. Lions begin to stalk. Hunt takes form of long circling tactic by two flank females. The rest walk straight in.

8:25 p.m. Attack is sprung. All lionesses run for the nearest zebras, randomly. One small foal narrowly escapes, puts on a late burst of energy, and outruns her pursuer. A good attempt but no kill.

8:30 p.m. Lionesses all greet and call softly and continue. One female gets sniffed in genitals by male, she growls and cuffs him in the face. He decides to leave her alone. They walk on.

8:53 p.m. Approximately half a mile from last hunt and two miles from shady tree they come across another herd of over 600 zebras and a fragmented group of 30 more zebras. In their midst are six impalas. The lions go into their crouching positions and stalk forward.

9:32 p.m. Their progress is slow because fragmented group of zebras keeps pushing the larger herd—probably because they are remnants of the last chased herd and they're alert. The trap is finally set off by the male, who runs at the impalas from a ridiculous distance. They spook and the lionesses all give up the hunt.

9:40 p.m. The last herd of zebras is still calling, so the lions start circling. One female goes a long way out to the left and then around behind the herd. The herd moves in a long line from left to right in front of a wall of waiting lionesses strung out, evenly spaced.

10:02 p.m. Lioness on the left runs in from ¾ angle behind the herd. It splits, some zebras running straight along their path (left to right), others breaking away toward the waiting lionesses. A lioness has got through their ranks and chases a mare and foal. They slip by her and dodge the male easily, duck through a gap between two standing lionesses, and off into the mass of striped horses. Another small group of zebras breaks towards the nearest lioness to us, ignores the vehicle and runs past. As the lioness sees them, she crouches and selects a victim. When they are only ten yards from her, she springs up and runs at another foal. The gap narrows and then suddenly widens. She gives up and looks over her shoulder and sees a lone stallion trotting through the gauntlet almost on top of a lioness, who leaps straight up and grabs the stallion with her front paws. The stallion bucks and sidesteps fast enough to throw the lioness off balance, and she goes down on her back into the grass. The zebra escapes, like all the zebras in this herd.

10:35 p.m. After greeting, to reassure each other that they are all O.K., and probably that no one made a kill quietly, they move off on another hunt.

11:14 p.m. After a long walk south, they find a herd of zebras walking in a long migration-type line. They circle ahead and most go straight in.

11:24 p.m. As they draw nearer, the herd of zebras suddenly takes flight. A hyena just blundered through.

11:31 p.m. They have all greeted and groomed a bit and are walking south. Odometer reading 4 ½ miles from the start of the night.

12:17 a.m. Zebra herds quite skittish now, but the lions stalk in to a herd that moves slowly ahead of them.

12:21 a.m. A wildebeest snorts, setting the herd of zebras, impalas, and wildebeests into a partial run. The lions try to get anything randomly. The wildebeests must have been lying down because they lag a bit behind the zebras. In the confusion a wildebeest calf falls down, but it's up in an instant and running to catch up. A lioness sees the opportunity and races in behind the calf. It separates itself by taking a sharp left turn. The lioness slips in the dewy grass and the calf turns again to join the herd. His new path takes him past the recovering lioness and she brings him down. A quick bite in the lower neck ends a life no more than two days long.

The buffalo seems to understand that running will invite attack while the lion waits either for a moment of weakness or for reinforcements. A single lion has little chance of success against a healthy buffalo bull.

12:25 a.m. All the lions run to the kill, but only the killer actually feeds.

12:26 a.m. The male runs in, a little late, and very aggressively takes the kill from the lioness, who doesn't argue but relinquishes her meal and trots away after the herd of zebras and wildebeests with the other lionesses.

12:28 a.m. They all stop and look back. The male is following without the kill. The lionesses turn to see what has happened to the meat. Two jackals are feeding on it. The male lion apparently didn't want to be left behind and so left the meat. They return and reclaim the carcass, but the male dominates again.

12:30 a.m. The lionesses wander off (westward) away from the herds they have been chasing.

12:40 a.m. Lionesses all stop, listen, and begin running.

12:45 a.m. They run toward the tree-line to the west of the marsh and stop. Very nervous and tense, they arrive at a kill with 19 other lions—Tshaba's group—feeding. It is an adult zebra. They don't go in to feed but wait, marking bushes, about 100 yards away.

1:00 a.m. The females from Maome's group lie down and watch Tshaba's group feeding.

1:40 a.m. The fighting on the carcass subsides, and individuals from Tshaba's group start leaving to lie down.

1:45 a.m. Maome's females start calling softly. Tshaba's group all look up, concerned. One young male leaves the carcass (there's now not much more than 20 percent of it left) and walks toward Maome's group. They all run away. He runs after them, not aggressively, more inquisitively.

1:55 a.m. All of Maome's pride stop running and roar deep, loud roars, simultaneously. Gaining confidence, they turn to face the young male, who runs away. They strut back toward the carcass.

2:00 a.m. All of Tshaba's group run, with four females from Maome's group in hot pursuit, roaring as they run and marking when they stop running. They chase Tshaba's whole pride of 19 into the thick mopane, without contact. Having successfully cleared the field, they head back to the carcass.

2:25 a.m. On the way back, one lioness stalks a hare, but it escapes.

2:41 a.m. Same lioness comes across four impalas grazing. She is joined by another lioness and they stalk the impalas. Impalas walk to within five yards before they see the lioness. She jumps, but they are too fast and escape as well.

2:54 a.m. Two lionesses return to the zebra carcass to find two other lionesses of their own pride feeding. The feeders growl aggressively as the chasers arrive.

3:09 a.m. Two more lionesses arrive. Unlike the previous two, they don't wait. All six jump in and feed and fight over the meal. One lioness gets a sharp cuff on top of her head, and the wound bleeds.

3:30 a.m. They all stop feeding and listen as a male and female lion start mating in the darkness not far from them. Then they feed on.

3:37 a.m. The mating couple arrives. She wants to feed. He wants to mate and stops any contact between her and her pride members. He growls at them and at her. She sneaks in very submissively toward the kill.

3:45 a.m. The male leaps at the feeding lionesses, grabs one, and slaps at her. She retaliates and claws his face. Blood flows. The six lionesses leave the kill, and the male and female feed tensely.

3:51 a.m. The lionesses of Maome's pride groom each other like kittens, licking each others' wounds and washing blood from the kill from each others' faces and necks.

4:12 a.m. They walk off toward zebras. The moon begins to glow through the clouds. Its light comes and goes.

4:19 a.m. They circle and attempt. One lioness comes in from the right, one from the left—all the others are asleep huddled together about 100 yards behind. It is a failure. The male lion that stole the wildebeest calf arrives and lies down with the sleepers.

4:40 a.m. The moon is bright with no clouds. They all sleep until 7:30 a.m., when dawn reveals that we are within sight of yesterday's shade tree.

8:40 a.m. They get up and walk to the tree.

10:00 a.m. We go off to sleep. When we return at 7:30 p.m. the lions still haven't moved!

In some parts of Africa lions avoid buffalo, but in others they are the ultimate challenge. A pride of eight females and subadults might wrestle a bull to the ground in just under an hour. This one took 2 ½ hours.

The African buffalo is a massive, powerful animal capable of inflicting mortal injuries on any attackers. These lions stay well to the rear of the bull's sweeping horns. Even so, a well-placed kick might break a jaw or a leg, either of which would mean a slow death from starvation.

Zebras migrate through Savuti twice each year, providing a feast for the lions. Ironically, this protects the zebra population since lions can only eat so many. Territorial predators such as lions depend less on migratory prey than on year-round resident species.

By October each water hole at Savuti has a resident pride of lions.

THE HUNT

After eight years of working with the lions, we had witnessed a wide variety of behavior. We had filmed almost everything they do both in the light and in the dark, but still we'd had no success filming daylight kills. In the hot summer of 1988, we followed Maome through the night. It had rained and we had been stuck in the mud for a few hours, but we'd managed to winch ourselves free. The lions stayed with us as we extricated the vehicle, and we all carried on again until dawn. The clouds cleared, leaving a humid dawn that developed into a stifling morning. Maome, Motsumi, Smudge, Thaka, and Slow Eyes were together; the other females were off with courting males. As they walked for the shade, heads hung low in the heat, they saw a bat-eared fox. Motsumi gave chase and, despite the heat, ran for over 500 yards, finally catching the fox and biting into its back. It was a pitiful end to a wet and tiring night.

The other lionesses caught up, but Motsumi had control and ran off with her catch. Soon, they all lost interest and abandoned the game and the fox for the shade of an acacia tree. When some tourists came by, we pointed the lions' hiding place out to them. Then we left to get a shower and some rest.

A few hours later, we met the tourists again. They thanked us profusely. They had found the lions, and, as we drove off, watched them sit up to observe some zebras pass by. With almost no stalking and very little effort, the lions hunted and caught a zebra within a few yards of the onlookers, all while we showered. The best opportunity in eight years.

Nobody ever said that this was going to be easy.

As I mentioned earlier, lions spend very little of their lives killing. In areas like Savuti, most of this behavior takes place at night, and with only a few exceptions it can truly be said that here they are nocturnal animals. It is indeed lucky to see them doing anything interesting during the day. We're always amazed at how different these lions are to those in East Africa,

To the uninitiated, porcupines may seem an easy meal; some will learn the hard way.

and are intrigued by the way the lions in Serengeti and Masai Mara carry on in the heat of the day, often not even seeking shade.

Some of the conclusions we've come to are a result of putting in the time, spending night after night with the lions. We witnessed over 1,300 kills, mainly at night (567 of those were with the same pride), and after watching so many hunts—well over 5,000 attempts—one can't help but learn something.

There are many factors that influence a hunt. The title *Hunting With the Moon* implies a conscious effort to take the effect of the moon into account; in fact, the most important thing we learned about the lions of Savuti is that they are extremely conscious of the moon.

As the moon brightens each night in the first half of the lunar month, lions increasingly use the dark parts of the night. From then on, through full moon until the last quarter, these lions pay special attention to when the moon is in the sky. Each night they hunt before it rises or after it sets, depending on the phase. Little or no hunting happens when a bright moon is in the night sky.

A half moon will remain in the sky for six hours after sunset, leaving the lions in bright moonlight until midnight, when the moon slips away and leaves the open marsh much darker. This is when the lions prefer to hunt. Plotting a graph of when the lions hunted during the night and when the moon set, we realized that the curves overlapped for the bright half of the month. Lions hunt as soon as the bright moon sets and before the bright moon rises.

The speed and maneuverability of ostriches make them difficult to catch most of the time, but lions will occasionally ambush one.

This became so obvious to us that if the moonset was in the second half of the evening, we could quite easily locate the lions at sunset, cook a meal on the exhaust manifold of the truck, eat, and bed down. Without fail, if we set the alarm clock to go off a few minutes before the moon's setting, we could wake, get warmly dressed, have a cup of tea, and be ready for the lions when they all got up to nuzzle one another into action and start moving off on the evening hunt.

On the other end of the scale, after full moon, the moon rises later into the night, which secures the early part of the night for dark hunting hours. Even if the lions haven't killed by eight or nine at night, when a bright moon emerges, they invariably give up, huddle together, and sleep.

During this time of the month we found that daylight sightings of lions were much fewer. They were simply in the thickly wooded mopane, hiding in the shade.

We figured this out by spending night after night with the lions, from sunset to sunrise and longer. It was only in 1985 that we were sure of their hunting-with-the-moon tactic—and there are always exceptions. One night, having just discovered this pattern, we watched the lions according to our moonset theory. Still quite pleased with ourselves, we found Maome's pride, ate, watched the lions until midnight, and then settled down for some sleep, sure that they would be there at 4:30 a.m. when the bright moon disappeared. At 3:30 a.m. I woke and decided to check on the lions, an automatic habit that usually means a quick look out at sleeping lions scattered all around within two or three yards of the vehicle. (They like to be near us in the winter if the engine is warm.)

The lions were all in front of the vehicle, but, to my amazement, they were feeding on a tsessebe! Somehow the animal must have wandered to within a few yards of the silent vehicle and its surrounding lions and got caught. We hadn't heard a thing.

Over 80 percent of the lion kills we recorded took place in the dark half of the moon's cycle. There are probably several reasons for this fact, some of which are fairly uncomplicated. Lions in Savuti have a very poor hunting success rate during the day. At night, the marsh is so open that during the full moon it might as well be daylight, even for us, and we have the worst night vision of any creature out there. With no cover, no shadows to hide in, the lions are noticed by the prey long before they can begin hunting effectively. Sometimes, if they are really hungry and the moon is against them, the lions turn away from the marsh where most of the animals are and hunt in the mopane forest that fringes the marsh. Here they find the shadows they need and hunt for the few animals that move in the dense bush at night.

Another factor often thought to be an influence on lions' hunting is the wind. From what we have seen, however, this is not the case. There is no circling downwind, with a male lion going upwind to scare the herds toward the females lying in ambush. Usually the males walk along behind, taking no notice of the females' hunting efforts, and often messing up the hunts by roaring from behind the females, sneezing at the wrong time, or sticking their noses up a stalking female's tail end to test for estrus—just as the lions are about to spring an ambush.

The wind can be a steady breeze from the northeast, as it often is, and the lions start hunting south or southwest, then turn east, circle around, and head west past where they slept during the day, changing direction randomly, according to an animal call, some wandering hyenas, another pride's roars, or any number of lion social responses.

It is true, however, that when the strong winds pick up from late August to October, just before the rains, lions do react differently.

The wind lifts the exposed dust of the dry season and mixes a thick cocktail in the air, stealing visibility and turning the mere act of looking out into a risky effort. Sand blows into eyes, ears, and nose. Lions tend to huddle together the way they do in the rain, facing into the dust. The males lie with closed eyes, but there is always one female among them with an open eye, and all have their ears alert.

Prey, like impalas and tsessebes, walk in long lines one behind another, looking only at the one ahead, facing also into the wind so that the gusts don't ruffle the hair on their skins. They tend to avoid the grassy areas, and so do the lions. If a line of impalas, wildebeests, tsessebes, or even zebras wanders past, the lions react immediately, using the confusion of the storm to hunt. When they hunt in these conditions, the visibility works against the prey and lions run in or wait in their path, leaping into action and causing more chaos. Of the hunts we saw, confusion-hunts like this brought

The migration trickles in with the first rains, and zebra calls fill the air with a sense of pandemonium.

Nomadic males must be skillful to hunt alone successfully and to keep their kills from being discovered. A noisy kill will attract resident male lions and their prides.

down a far greater percentage of multiple kills. The lions would run in from all sides killing prey, often one per lion. Eight lionesses and a male, all from Maome's pride, killed seven impalas one night. As the impalas scattered, another and then another golden shadow would loom up out of the dust at their feet. As far as we know, this is the only type of wind-related hunting they ever did, and, in fact, they used the opportunity the wind provided them, not the wind itself.

Hyenas do exactly the same. On windy August days, they suddenly turn to warthog hunting for a week. Small bands of hyenas walk across the marsh, giving chase to warthogs—an activity they wouldn't even consider any other time of the year.

The moon also affects hyenas, although to a lesser degree. We have never seen a hyena hunt during a full moon, and although our hyena hunting figures are far smaller than our lion observations (hyena kills recorded are around the 350 mark), 70 percent of those were in the dark phase.

Rain is another factor to consider. Much to our discomfort, the lions don't mind hunting in the rain, unless it buckets down, in which case they stop everything and find an open area to huddle together in. Seldom do they seek shelter under trees, unless they are near some *Acacia hebaclada* that form solid, low umbrellas of thorns and leaves. If the heavy downpour lets up, they will go out looking for prey. Our discomfort comes because we will have to follow in a vehicle with a huge tarpaulin tied over it to cover the roof hatch, and the windshield in the up position, which is almost never the case otherwise. There isn't much we can do about the doors. When we arrive in the bush from town, we remove them and mount camera heads and other equipment hardware in their place. To refit them in the wet season would be too problematic, so water gushes in through the sides, drenching the two of us. The equipment stays in its boxes until the last moment of action to keep it dry, and lights that usually mount through the roof bounce about out of control in the cab with us. It is probably of some significance that we haven't filmed anything unusually spectacular in heavy rain, and we normally end up shivering in wet clothes, huddled in the back under the tarpaulin, with a mug of hot tea if we're lucky.

Like the windstorms, rain serves the lions more as a catalyst for confusion than anything else, a confusion from which the lions can profit. In the rainy season the zebras are around Savuti, and they are the most likely prey. Zebras behave less stupidly in extreme weather than impalas and tsessebes do, so hunting is more difficult. Lions go skidding off in the mud if a zebra takes a sharp turn while being chased. During one kill we watched in the rain, a young wildebeest was separated and ran off with the zebras when the lions spooked the combined herd. As the wildebeest was singled out, the zebra herd broke suddenly to the right, and most of the lions slipped around like first-time skaters on ice. One lioness was locked onto the wildebeest and pursued it, reaching out at its heels with each forward bound. Finally the lioness (Slow Eyes) caught up and hooked the young wildebeest, and the two figures slid together on the wet grass for over 20 yards.

We need a little lead time to prepare our vehicle for a storm. Late one November, we were filming some mating lions at sunset. A storm advanced from behind them, and we tried to get the mating with lightning behind the lions. I had a bad case of malaria, which didn't halt the work but made decisions a little more difficult. We also find that during the long dry season, we both forget so easily the ferocity of the storms. When Beverly suggested closing up, I said I didn't think it would come our way. I was wrong. Before we could even get the windshield up, it was raining. The wind whipped the canvas around madly, making it impossible to tie it down. Rain bucketed down on us, and our own raincoats were hidden somewhere below our dry-season clothes. Beverly had to stay inside the vehicle saving camera equipment as inches of water filled the truck. The vehicle rocked in the wind and looked as though it might even tip over. On the roof I could no longer communicate with Beverly; I gave up the struggle to sort out the ropes, and opted instead to lie spread-eagle on the canvas that covered the roof to protect the inside from getting even more drenched. I was soaked anyway. The wind got in under the canvas and jerked it up violently, throwing me up in the air and to one side. The only thing that saved me from trampolining from the roof to the ground was a corner rope on the tarpaulin that had wound itself around

After nine rainless months, November brings storms that signal a change for the lions: new strategies and different prey.

my ankle. This jerked me back into position.

Finally, the wind let up briefly, and Beverly, who by now had secured the equipment and excavated the rain gear, climbed out of the car and roped down a corner, which was enough to anchor the whole contraption so that I could tie down the other corners. Somehow we managed to get ourselves sorted out and climbed back inside. It was like a shipwreck. Buckets of water kept washing over us. Like two drowned rats, we sat huddled in the back, our feet in a few inches of water, looking, no doubt, fairly miserable. The rain stopped and we peered out. The two lions carried on mating as if nothing had happened. Our view of them was a bit askew: somehow we had managed to get a flat tire, without even moving!

Temperature became a second breakthrough for us. After years of watching the lions, we noticed an interesting pattern of reactions to temperature changes. If we were with lions that were sleeping, even on a dark night, and we felt a sudden temperature drop that necessitated an extra sweater or jacket, the lions would get up and prompt each other into movement. The hunting would begin. We decided to experiment, keeping a thermometer taped to the dashboard. It seemed that every dark night around 2:00 a.m. the temperature dropped just a little. That sudden drop was enough to spark the lions into action. We correlated the temperature drops to lion activity patterns and found a surprising parallel.

Lions have relatively small, inefficient hearts, the reason for their poor performance when it's hot, as it is during the day in Savuti. The drop in temperature gives them the slight advantage they need to hunt fast-moving prey like tsessebes, the fastest antelopes in Africa. And they do hunt tsessebes quite successfully in Savuti. In fact, for many months during the dry winter, that is all they eat, except for the occasional impala.

Rains fall in November, after a long dry season of nine months. All the zebras that concentrate along the Linyanti river system start to move southeast. In late November, or about two weeks after the first good rains, they pour into Savuti, and it is then that I can't get the words "flying hooves, golden shadows" out of my head. The phrase is the title of a book by George Schaller, and it has haunted me for 20 years because it exactly describes what happens when the zebras arrive in Savuti and the lions shadow their every move. By then the lions have been through seven months of struggling to eat impalas, tsessebes, or wildebeests, sometimes scavenging off elephant carcasses. The first distant staccato calls of the zebras set off a wave of excitement.

There are few more dramatically graphic symbols of Africa than the zebra, whose dazzling stripes are the most unlikely camouflage in this often bleak landscape. Both Beverly and I were so captivated by these animals that we decided to make a film about them. We called it *Patterns in the Grass*, not only because of the zebra's distinctive skins but because of the complicated pattern of migration paths we saw one day from our friend Lloyd Wilmot's small Cessna.

We flew above the zebras at 200 feet. Lloyd turned the nose into the wind and put down full flaps, and the plane stopped. Although

The onset of the rainy season disperses prey that previously never wandered far from the water holes.

still flying, we were stationary in relation to the ground, like a helicopter. From this rather unreal perch, with the passenger door removed, I had the almost irresistible urge to simply step out into "miniature land" where the lush green marsh spread out below and long lines of zebras were visible only because their shadows lay flat out next to them, easily ten times the length of a zebra's height. Behind them a long winding path stretched forever into the greenery, and ahead the route was clearly marked. Countless herds and family groups had used this same path for so many years that time ridiculed any attempt to age them. These were the real patterns in the grass, along which every zebra walked in single file.

Often it takes the lions and hyenas a few days to react to the influx of zebra before the hunting begins. When it does, the marsh is flooded with zebra cries, desperate contact calls as they try to keep together, and stampeding hooves.

Lions cannot live on zebra alone. No predator can sustain itself on a passing migration, and it is the quiet season supply of food that determines how many the area can support. In an effort to find out how much is eaten and what proportion is made up by zebras, we followed both predator and prey for years.

Not all lion hunting stories are successes. In fact, most hunts are unsuccessful. On average we would watch four unsuccessful hunts to every good one. If hunting success is the criterion, then as a rule lions are relatively poor predators, compared with wild dogs, hyenas, and cheetahs. Even leopards are better than lions when you compare the ratio of attempted kills to successful kills. (Of course, if proliferation is the success badge of a species, lions do better than most.) With an animal like the tsessebe, success rates are even lower, especially during the day. Usually tsessebes outrun lions, even at night. The only way for lions to catch tsessebes (unless they have a freak burst of energy!) is by circling around, possibly in a "pincer" movement, then giving chase, creating chaos, and taking whatever comes by.

We have watched many hundreds of attempts to catch warthogs during the winter days. In Savuti, which now verges on semi-desert in the dry season, winter means night temperatures below freezing, but day temperatures of anything up to 120 degrees. By 10:00 a.m. the heat is unbearable, especially because of the contrast with the night, and yet on some days the lions still hunt warthogs.

Maome's group would spot a few warthogs rooting for the succulent rhizomes of the cynodon grasses that grow on the marsh. These cynodon grasses keep moisture in their root system well into the winter. The lions would go into an exceptionally long maneuver, fanning out across the marsh often miles apart, homing in on the unaware warthogs. Every now and again one of the pigs would lift its head or come up off its knees and survey the area, and the lions would freeze or flatten themselves.

Day stalking is different from night stalking. In the bright light a lioness stalks with her head less than two inches from the ground, her body not rising and falling but gliding, as if propelled by some motorized force from behind. The only movement is her shoulder blades pumping away carefully. Her legs are hidden by the grass. From warthog height only a straight tawny back, if anything, protrudes from the grass. The difference is that the whole play can be seen in the daylight hours, as opposed to the glimpses and surprises of the nocturnal hunts. A typical photograph of lions hunting during the day shows one lioness low in the grass. Night stalking, on the other hand, is bolder. The lions move upright. They stay together longer, and they get closer to the prey before splitting up to attack. A typical shot of lions hunting at night shows all the lionesses together—a long line of eyes glowing in the dark.

When it comes to hunting warthogs in Savuti, the kill rate for lions is considerably lower than average—perhaps one in every 20 attempts succeeds. Mostly the lions seemed to invest their last morning hours in a hunt that ended with the warthogs jumping up from their kneeling position, alerted by something very subtle like a faint smell of predators or a shuffling in the grass as the lions drew nearer. Warthogs' eyes are placed deceivingly high on their heads; when they feed, their heads are lowered, so one imagines them to be occupied, but those eyes are facing outward, watching for the horizon to suddenly acquire two tawny ears. The slightest hint of danger sends them off at top speed.

Hours would go by as we waited and watched these unsuccessful hunts, and often so would the tourists. They were mostly very careful about approaching. No one could mistake the serious posture of a stalking lion, and everyone is fascinated by the prospect of blood,

While males will often not allow females to share a kill, cubs are tolerated.

A kudu bull will provide a two-day meal for this nomadic lioness, if she can keep it.

especially that of "an ugly little pig." Of course, warthogs are low on the human appreciation scale, but Maome's lionesses probably judge each species by a different set of criteria. How fast are they, how big are they, how difficult are they to kill?

One of the most important things we've learned about lions is that they are highly individual. A lioness can prefer to hunt warthogs and do so very efficiently. One can be a buffalo specialist, another an expert elephant hunter. On the occasions when buffalo are "in season," those lionesses who know how to hunt them will lead the attack on the herd's seemingly impenetrable phalanx of muscle and horn. In winter, when long daytime hunts of warthog take place, one or two specialist lions seem to initiate the hunts, often with other females following begrudgingly behind and going through the motions of stalking—but seldom actually catching their prey.

In hunts that involve wildebeests and zebras, which are almost staples—all the lionesses seem to do equally well at these—we found a pattern in their tactics and noticed that the same lionesses took the same positions night after night. Maome, for example, always chose the left flank over the right. Was this because she had a weaker left eye? Could she have been "right handed"? We can't answer these questions yet. For now, we can only recognize the intriguing patterns, and hope that further research will make their meaning clear.

A tortoise provides a momentary diversion for an inquisitive cub.

After a large kill, the lionesses will often move their cubs to the carcass while it lasts.

AGAINST THE ODDS

In Savuti, lions typically hunt buffalo and zebras, along with wildebeests and, of course, impalas. Warthogs are less commonly and less successfully hunted, as described. But lions have an even lower success rate for hunting another species. Strangely, this species provided the lions of Savuti with about 20 percent of their total food in 1990.

To hunt this prey, lions have to have the experience of generations of specific hunting techniques. Many don't have the skill. No doubt some will never even attempt it. But for those that do try and succeed, the reward is great—as is the risk.

Only one animal can test a lion's skill so thoroughly. Elephants!

The hunting of elephants by lions is comparatively rare. It stands to reason that leaping onto the thick hide of an adult elephant's back would be fairly useless, but lions do risk actual hunts into large breeding herds of bulls, cows, and calves. In fact, we have been seeing more and more elephant hunts in Botswana. There is a valley called Nxwazumba, to the northeast of Savuti, where the elephants dominate the water holes and are the lions' main prey.

The elephant-hunting approach is direct, much like the approach to hunting buffalo, and is followed by a straight-in charge. No stealthy stalking here. This very visible attack is most effective in spooking the herds, and as a herd bunches and panics, the confusion is their downfall. Calves are separated, and sometimes they are knocked over. If the lions keep up a vocal and aggressive inward thrust, the herd will keep going. Most times a calf's calls will turn the whole herd or at least the mother and her nearest kin, but often it is too late.

Without a doubt this is the hardest lion kill to witness. As much as we force our objectivity to the fore and even verbally encourage each other not to be emotional, both Beverly and I have been devastated by the cries of the calf and the confusion of the mother, desperate to get to her dying young.

Once again we must consider what is right and what is wrong. For us, the only definite wrong would be to interfere in this ancient, admittedly sad, struggle. At times in Nxwazumba, the lions have no other food supply but elephants, and without that moment of intense harshness, they would suffer a lingering death by starvation.

In Savuti the lions are less adept at handling the elephant herds, but as always they are the consummate opportunists.

Because we were working on a concurrent project on elephants, we made it our task to identify all the bull elephants in Savuti. Breeding herds were done as well, but their presence is rare in Savuti, and we seldom see the same herd return. In July of 1990 we were following an old bull. He was desperately thin and looked like he would fade away to dust any moment. Often while others fought and jostled around the water hole, he stood in the sun, not bothering to move just the few yards into the shade. With the sunlight constantly on his gaunt back, he struck a haunting pose. The mud on his body dried to a fine white powder and flaked off in places. He so looked like Merlin in his ghostly form that it was difficult not to refer to him with reverence.

It is at times like these that friendly tip-offs from tour operators really help. Our friend June Wilmot radioed us in when the old bull was on his last legs.

One day he could resist the call of the water no longer and ventured in among the jostling bulls. He was no match for them, and a jagged tusk stabbed him fatally in the neck. During his last moments and shortly after his death the younger bulls in the group engaged in some very strange behavior. What initially looked to us like an investigation of the fallen elephant became much more. The first young bull started rubbing his chest on the rump of the old elephant. Then after a few minutes he climbed up onto the body in the typical mating fashion. Although this mock mating took over a minute, the surrounding bulls took no notice at all. Only the waiting hyenas watched from the shadows of a full moon.

The only conclusion I can come to about the mock mating behavior is that it was a dominance display designed to elevate the young bull's status in the strict hierarchy. If the young bull was ranked 120th and he dominated the old bull, who was ranked 40th, then presumably he would climb beyond or at least close to that, if only temporarily.

The stakeout was as revealing for the lion and hyena interactions around the carcass as it was for the elephant interactions.

Two prides of lions and two clans of hyenas, together with perhaps 40 vultures, devoured most of the meat during the eight-day and eight-night watch. The lions arrived the first few days and chased the hyenas off. The hyenas rallied and succeeded in winning the carcass again, just in time to relinquish it to a neighboring clan after a spectacular battle. Finally another pride of lions took possession, fought off the hyenas of both clans, chased other lions away, and settled in for the duration. From that time on the transformation from huge carcass to scattered bones in the dust was very rapid.

Throughout all this the elephant bulls visited the carcass constantly. Sometimes they gathered around the remains and did nothing

Having tasted the blood of the calf, the lions will not be spooked by elephants defending a lost cause.

but stand there silently, unmoving, for up to 15 minutes at a time. Often they gathered and smelled every part of the body with delicate movements of their trunks, gliding just a fraction away from actual touch. The silent gatherings were the most unsettling, and we had to quell feelings of guilt about intruding on what looked like a private moment. In the three-quarter moonlight, which was bright enough to allow us to see detail without lights, there was something haunting about watching a group of elephants float silently up to the remains of one of their companions, stand around in a group doing nothing, and then vanish again, their grey shapes melting into the darkness.

We had always wanted to document exactly what happens to a carcass from the moment of death to the dry bones stage. On film a record of this allows the approximation of what each phase of scavenging consumes, and although it is not as accurate as weighing the remains after each scavenger leaves, it is less disturbing.

By the time the carcass was down to bone, Beverly was sick to her stomach but hanging in there like a trooper. The people of Lloyd's camp, who had been bringing us boiled water for tea from time to time, suggested that we come in to their camp for a meal. It was a welcome invitation. We'd had quite enough of living in the constant stench of decaying flesh.

When we arrived, June Wilmot greeted us with her usual friendliness, which immediately changed to a sudden withdrawal, followed by the offer of—no, the insistence upon—a shower. The elephant smell had collected on our bodies, clothing, and hair. Because of our familiarity with the odor we hadn't noticed. We also hadn't noticed, at least at the time, that the tourists were giving us a wide berth.

The lions were stuffed full of elephant meat and could hardly move. Clouds came over and the prospect of filming was non-existent. The stakeout was officially declared over, and we headed for our camp. We'd been back only a few hours when we got the radio message. The lions had killed a giraffe at the water hole. I couldn't believe it! The only way they could have killed anything, I thought, was by rolling over on it. We packed and headed straight back to Savuti. We arrived at night once again, to a sight that in our exhausted state could only make us sit back and laugh.

The giraffe had been eaten completely. Only a few bones remained. One hyena chewed on a leg. In the shade a bundle of lions lay, so bloated that their enlarged white bellies looked like a series of termite mounds in the grass. Not one moved. Occasionally the panting of one would stop, and it would hold its breath, and then a loud explosion of gas would leave its body at the tail end, smelling very like the elephant carcass of the day before.

Never before had we arrived at a party so late. Some way off, we settled down to sleep ourselves, both exhausted.

At midnight my alarm went off. I checked the bundle of lions. All quite still, apart from the constant rise and fall of bloated bellies. Gentle snores emanated from a half a dozen throats. Behind us I was aware of a breeding herd of elephants drinking among the bull elephants. Hyenas were being chased, a young

The death of an elephant is a memorable event in the life of the herd. Survivors congregate for days, sometimes in silence and without touching.

A lower-ranking bull 'mock mates' his fallen companion, perhaps in an attempt to claim dominance and increase his status.

We were initially astounded by evidence that lions attacked and killed elephants. As we became better at keeping up with the prides and as the lions became more familiar with the presence of elephant herds, we recorded more and more elephant kills.

Lion predation of elephants occurs most often at night. In this unusual instance of a daylight attack, the calf had been left behind inadvertently by the herd.

elephant was bellowing but soon stopped. The lions didn't even cock an ear.

At 2:00 a.m. the alarm sounded again. Lions still slept. Elephants were quieter but still active. At around 3:30 a.m., in my sleep, I heard heavy panting. Something ran past the vehicle close enough to touch, and then it was quiet. I drifted off again momentarily and then jumped up, rousing Beverly. "They're on an elephant!" I yelled.

I turned the truck and within 30 feet of us our lights picked up the final moments of the attack. A six-year-old calf was standing splay-legged, apparently determined not to be bowled over. A lioness, almost the size of the elephant, had her front feet up on its rump and was biting into the lower backbone. She wasn't being very effective. Another lioness got clobbered by the trunk and rolled over on her back at the feet of the elephant. These were amateur elephant hunters. Two males circled, staying out of trouble. Another female jumped against the calf's side but bounced straight off. Suddenly, as if realizing from the female's actions that this was a worthwhile tactic, a male ran straight into the side of the young elephant. The impact knocked the wind out of the little elephant and it went down. Immediately the lionesses were on it.

One female coming to the front end got whacked by the trunk and jumped away. The lioness on the throat was being beaten by the trunk so she released her grip and grabbed the trunk. Finally, after some time, a second lioness took over at the throat.

Strangely, no mother came to the calf's

Disturbing though it is, lion predation of elephants is as natural as any predator/prey relationship. The ease with which lions have taken up the hunting of elephants suggests that it is not a new phenomenon. Most kills are young elephants, but we have witnessed lions bringing down full-grown elephants as well.

aid. Perhaps his mother had a newer calf to protect, or maybe he'd gotten separated from the herd before the lions found him.

After the calf had been silent for a reasonable length of time, when we presumed that death had claimed its victim, we drove right up to the calf to get a sex and age estimate for later scientific record. (By now the lions had accepted us so totally that we could have pulled on one end of the kill.) As we approached to within a yard of the head, I could see into the eye of the calf. Feebly he raised his trunk toward us. The unscientific half of my brain will remember that image forever.

We backed off immediately, fearing that our presence would prolong a process we had mistakenly thought was long over.

In the late dry season, the water hole at Savuti becomes the focal point, and it is here that the Savuti lions gain their familiarity with elephants. Each day they have to sneak through the giant legs to get a precious drink. Fortunately for them, if they are killing readily, blood and moisture in the carcasses sates their thirsts. For the elephants, who consume tons of dry plant material, water is a necessity.

One memorable day, a prime male lion watched a breeding herd with a newly born elephant calf struggling in the mud of the water hole. He was not particularly interested. He had come for water, and the black muddy patch on his chin indicated that he had been successful in drinking. This lion had a strong character, and, because of an incident I'll describe later, we named him Ntchwaidumela—"he who greets with fire." In all else he deferred to his companion, who was probably a half brother or first cousin, but he was certainly stout of heart when it came to confrontations with other species, elephants included.

As Ntchwaidumela rested near the water, two huge bulls came down to drink. He virtually ignored them as they thundered slowly past, within ten feet of him. Suddenly the second bull saw the lion and bellowed, fanning out his ears. Usually this would have got anything up and running, but Ntchwaidumela actually looked the other way. Then the elephant charged, and in a second the lion whipped around and charged right back, leaping up at the bull elephant's head. The elephant stopped, but before the dust could settle he kicked out at the male lion, who was back in the resting position, looking at his adversary. The bull stepped forward again, determined to see the lion off. Now, with less than a yard between him and the elephant, the lion still growled, and he stood down the charge until the very last second, when he ducked away under the massive feet. The interaction over, the elephant moved off, and Ntchwaidumela settled defiantly down to rest again no more than 30 feet away. Over the years, this male lion lived up to his name many times.

In May of 1991 we had an ideal chance to watch another carcass and once again document almost by the mouthful what happens to a huge elephant after death. This occurrence was particularly spectacular because it was miles into the bush where no one goes, and the elephant had died right in the middle of a rainwater pan. I will always remember one night at his carcass.

Ntchwaidumela confronts a bull elephant.

A lioness from Maome's pride claims the carcass of an elephant that died in the midst of a rain pan, a grey island of meat.

The moon was just smaller than half, a silver sickle poised ready to slice into the bush, and it moved slowly toward the jagged horizon of mopane treetops. In the soft blue light of night I sat on the damp ground close to the water's edge. Beverly had parked the Land Cruiser with all her equipment and lights about 100 yards away on the other side of the water. I had a second vehicle parked not too far behind me but sat stretched out under a tripod on the ground waiting for something to come in to feed. The legs of the tripod were so cold that they almost burned my skin, and the damp was eating its way into my body. The experience of being out on the ground surrounded only by darkness was overpowering all other sensations.

As I waited silently I eased my muscles against their boredom, stretching out very slowly backward. My hand sliding along the white sand went into something soft and wet, either hyena droppings or an abandoned piece of meat from the elephant carcass. Everything was quiet, although I could hear the occasional dung beetle fly into the other vehicle. Beverly also waited motionlessly.

I felt some shapes go by before I heard the soft crunching of the sand. A dark hyena's body moved up to the water's edge.

They were obviously a little wary of my presence, a new shape to them, the scent and outline usually associated with a vehicle now alone on the white sand. They overcame their concerns quickly and waded into the water

A huge protein source in the form of a dead bull elephant is quickly recycled by predators and scavengers.

to the huge feast that beckoned them. As they got to the carcass they dropped all pretenses and dived into a feeding frenzy, splashing as they squabbled over bits and pieces. (It is incredible that with a few tons of meat in front of them they still fight over scraps.) Beverly put the filming light on, and the solid black images rimmed with white backlight were haunting. The splashes in the water picked up the light and sparkles of light danced around the legs and submerged feet of the hyenas as they ripped away at the dormant hulk of what was once a bull elephant. From my perspective, down low on the ground, the hyenas looked unreal, much larger than usual. Without light on their features they could easily have been the wolves, wild dogs, or hyena-type creatures of our nightmares. In that haunting light the blood drooling out of their mouths lost its importance and became colorless, although in my mind I could piece together the visual and the imagined information. They were 20 paces from me. By now hyenas were everywhere. I could hear them in the bushes behind me, to the left and on the other side of the water hole. Every now and then one came into the water to join the feed, which had reached such a high level of sound that Beverly and I could only communicate by a series of tiny flashlight signals.

From time to time a curious newcomer would come up behind me, cutting off my escape route to the second vehicle, but its intentions were easy to read, and when the wet nose touched my finger on the hand that braced my body, the hyena jumped back at the realization of what I was. When he returned for another sniff I sat upright, and he loped off, circled, and went into the water to feed.

Suddenly the alarm went out, like water bursting through an air-filled pipe. A moment's silence and then the hyenas ran for cover. Both Beverly and I got shots of them racing through the water to escape the phantoms of their imagination. They had been doing this on and off the whole night; after each confused evacuation of the carcass, the disturbed water slowly settled against the shore, and the heavy silence dropped down over us all again. During these moments the pressure of silence on my eardrums played tricks on my mind. It felt like I was in the engine room of a great sea vessel, the constant drone of engine noise deafeningly monotonous. It is only when that silence is violated by a tiny twig being snapped that perspective returns, the tiny noise sounding like the explosion of dynamite in the engine room of sound.

This time the hyenas' phantom was real. Another creature was stalking the water hole. Beverly flicked on the spotlight and picked up the movement. A tawny shape glided from the cover of one bush to another, then emerged just behind me. The light went off, and after my eyes adjusted to the darkness I looked at the lioness. Against the white sand her golden coat looked black, a silhouette that betrayed her almost perfect camouflage in other conditions. Slowly she circled the water, trying at various spots to get in to the elephant, but she retreated each time, hissing at the obstacle that glistened in the moonlight. When she put her foot into the water she quickly backed out growling. She circled again.

Beverly said, just loud enough for me to hear her across the icy water, "We know her. She's from Maome's pride."

I relaxed a bit at this news. I knew that a strange lioness would have been frightened to find me out of my vehicle.

Soon she had nearly completed the circle, which brought her straight toward me. She hesitated a yard away. My head was below her eye level, a wonderful sensation. The soft light from Beverly's flashlight went on, and the lioness looked at this strange creature with shiny metal parts sprawled in front of her. I'm sure that she wasn't confused. To a lion we must smell very strongly of what we are.

She stepped around me to continue her quest for a way to the carcass. As she did so she put her foot into the water, and in a fright jumped to her left, bumping into the tripod and standing on my foot in the process.

I dropped down to the ground and turned my vulnerable face, chest, and stomach away from her, prepared for the worst. My reaction startled her, and she jumped away, back into the water. The shock of the cold water made her growl and step back again swiftly. I turned to face her. Not wanting to make contact, she deftly sprang over my lower body and avoided both the water and me.

As it got light, the lioness finally braved the water. She chased the hyenas and vultures away and fed, standing on the elephant to keep her feet dry.

Three subadults of 2 ½ years are the makings of a new coalition and a hope for the future.

Savuti's isolated water holes become eerily chaotic with wildlife in the late dry season when everything is parched and desperate for moisture.

Elephants, massing in huge clans, move together along ancient trails toward the rivers.

ETERNAL ENEMIES

One characteristic that makes it difficult to love hyenas is their ability to find weaknesses in your camp or vehicle. Savuti is notorious for camp hyenas that steal food, boxes that once had food in them, boxes or trunks that once touched boxes that once had food in them, and even items that might have touched a trunk near a box of food, or soap. They also steal anything else. They break into refrigerators, reed structures, and sometimes tents. They chew anything. At one camp in Savuti, a hyena bit into the liquid gas pipe to the refrigerator. The gas escaped onto the open flame, ignited, and exploded the propane gas cylinder into a ball of fire. The whole main structure of the camp burned to the ground. The most important loss to the manager was his entire collection of photographs from his bush career. (I don't know what happened to the hyena!)

One day, after a particularly good run of filming during which we documented, quite clearly, the nighttime killing of a zebra by hyenas, one of these camp hyenas got into our reed hut. We had abandoned our tent a few months before when an elephant walked over it, smashing all the poles, the bed, the cupboards, and the canvas sides. The 15-by-15-foot reed hut then became our only home for about eight months. The hyena smashed through the door and jumped into the fridge, once he had chewed off the lid. We were out as usual that night and returned to discover the mess strewn around; from the tracks we could reconstruct the scene of the crime. He had sat inside the freezer chewing cheese, the only food item in the freezer, and finally left with a mouthful of film cans. All the film we had shot over the previous two weeks went out with him, including the very incriminating film of the hyenas killing a zebra. We searched the surrounding area and finally found all of the film cans, all except Roll 14, the "kill roll." By midday we had collected all the debris. We did one last circuit and Beverly discovered the missing can in the bright sun with one clear mark where a tooth had pierced the tin can. We were sure the footage was exposed to light, or at least heat, but decided to include it in the next batch to be sent to the lab. We didn't mark the cans for any special attention and eagerly awaited a lab report. A few days later we received a radio message: "All film fine, processed as normal" with an additional, "What do you people do to your film cans—feed them to lions?"

As things became clearer to us, we became more interested in the hyenas and the clan system in Savuti. Hyenas are fascinating, and not only because of their strange behavior and strange ancestry. (They are not dogs, but are in fact more closely related to viverrids, a family that includes mongoose, badgers, and ferrets.) They are able to transform themselves instantly from sleepy, trusting, puppy-dog-like animals to alert predators. In this predator phase, they stand high on their legs, often running in, bobbing up and down to see over the grass, eyes fixed on one prey but ready to change if the situation presents an easier victim. This transition is so much faster than with lions, who normally go through the sleep to hunt phases quite gradually, unless opportunity sends them a surprise.

Hyenas live on opportunity. At once you can enjoy their intricate social bounds within the clan and be astounded by the viciousness of their feeding frenzies. They have a reputation for being cowardly, a human characterization that has unclear origins. It is interesting that when we talk to people from all spheres of life who are not avid wildlife enthusiasts (and even some that are), the mere mention of a hyena makes them turn up their noses and say something like "those smelly, evil, dirty scavengers." Actually hyenas spend a lot of time grooming themselves and each other. Like the lions, who always look clean, they have their moments. (We have seen lions eating among maggots from an elephant carcass.) Hyenas do scavenge, but many hundreds of times we have seen lions run in to scavenge from the hyenas.

If we categorize predators and subdivide them again, two stand out above the rest as superpredators: lions and hyenas. Both can bring down buffalo, the largest prey regularly available to them. It was within days of our arrival in Savuti that we first witnessed the astonishing enmity that exists there between these two superpredators.

On our seventh night in Savuti, we were with a group of seven young lionesses as they caught a young steenbok by chance, and within four minutes it was as if the animal had never existed. Next they proceeded toward their main goal, a zebra herd in the distance. The stalk and hunt were successful; a young zebra foal was isolated from the herd and secured. One lioness held it firmly by the throat and the others began to eat from around the face and neck. Because of the thick vegetation, the lions were scattered, and not all had found the kill by the time the first hyenas arrived. The very humanlike cry of the captured foal persisted through all this activity, clearly indicating

This elephant died of natural causes in a water hole. Over the next ten days vultures, hyenas, lions, jackals, and a host of other scavengers devoured the 11-ton carcass.

that it had not yet succumbed to the tranquility of death. The howls and eerie cackles of the hyenas preceded them from the darkness, and the lions flattened their ears and ate faster, only occasionally looking up as the clan's numbers grew. It was a sound recordist's paradise, a crazy cacophony of sounds that Beverly later became expert at capturing.

Within minutes, the foal's calls were joined by the crazed whooping calls of 30 or 40 hyenas. Time passed in slow motion, as it tends to on memorable occasions. The lead hyenas launched their attack on the lions, engulfing them in a sea of jaws and tough spotted skins. The lionesses could do little but protect themselves, and they abandoned their kill. The hyenas, intent on a good margin of dominance, chased the lions away for 50 yards and in their enthusiasm failed to notice that the young zebra foal was up on its feet again, a lot worse for wear but about to make off. The scene was like the animal equivalent of *Phantom of the Opera* or the Wax Museum, only more horrific. This "half-zebra" resurrected from the dead thankfully lasted only a few seconds on its feet until a frenzied passing hyena bowled it over again and set about disemboweling it. The painful screeching ceased. Hyenas tumbled back into our field of light from the left, one or two with lion blood on their lips.

No sooner were most of the hyenas back than a warning babbling noise started among them, and they all immediately stood back and scanned for danger. They froze and were silent momentarily until a huge hyena burst through the wild sage from the right. She was closely followed by many others, and, as we shone our spotlights, the eyes bobbed like an armada at night. Another 30 or 40 hyenas ran toward the carcass of the zebra foal at full speed, all with their tails up and fluffed out, a typical aggressive display. Dust swirled, and it was becoming more difficult to see or understand the situation. As this lead female appeared with her mob, the feeding hyenas scattered, and it seemed as though we and the carcass were at the center of a border dispute between the two large clans of hyenas in the area.

Eighty hyenas darted and ran, some through bushes and trees, snapping and howling. Teeth were bared by all pursuers and pursued. Those slow to escape were mobbed and bitten. Blood flowed and dust swirled, and then, impossibly, as if it were a symbol of the horror, the zebra foal raised itself to its feet again and tried to make another escape. By now more than half of its weight had been consumed. Medically, I imagine, it should have been impossible—in the dust one could have been forgiven for believing in ghosts.

Once again in the confusion the foal was swept up and the new clan descended on it. Before long the alarm call babble went out again and the new clan retreated with their tails up, for a few seconds, surrendering their carcass to the original clan. Only one or two fed before they were solidly ousted a second time by the big female and her clan. The zebra foal was devoured in a flurry by the final victors of the war.

We both sat riveted, not saying a printable word. We felt totally drained by the experience. It was our first hyena takeover, the first of over 200. I looked down at my watch: the entire episode had taken 14 minutes! It was the shortest battle in any war I have known. The lions, whom we caught up with a little later, limped away to find a quiet place to lick their wounds.

Since then I can truly say we have been prepared for anything, no horror too unspeakable, no kill, no violence unexpectedly harsh. In fact, and I say this with some thought, we have come to enjoy our impartiality to Africa's nocturnal harshness. This doesn't mean that we enjoy the death and suffering, but that we can do our work as observers, as filmmakers and documenters rather than emotional participants. Ours is a difficult role, though, in one basic way. We are expected to be impartial witnesses of nature's ancient methods of survival, and yet we need to add our interpretations to the events because we presumably know more about what happens than other viewers. Add to that recipe a healthy dose of passion and emotion, because without it, who cares, and who will care for the films we produce or the place we care for so much? So we live this life of contradiction. The other contradiction is that we are on a constant quest for new areas, new wildernesses in which to work, film, and produce. These produc-

A solitary lioness will be driven from her kill by hyenas made bold by their numbers.

tions, however, can popularize areas. People then focus their attention on them, and that wilderness can be lost. And we have to continue our destructive quest.

It is a rare privilege to know that from time to time a film does influence the right people, and perhaps save an area or help conserve a species. This motivation keeps us going.

Very quickly we realized that what was happening in Savuti was very special from an observer's point of view. These hyena-lion clashes happen almost everywhere where lions and hyenas are in large enough numbers, but in places like the Masai Mara a lot of the lion hunting happens during the day. Some hyena takeovers have been seen, but it was quite stunning that when we did eventually release a film on this relationship, the strongest reaction came from people in East Africa, who could not believe the intensity of these interactions. In East Africa, apparently, these two animals enjoy a harmonious relationship by comparison. There they share the same shade! In most parts of Botswana only a dead hyena would share shade with a lion.

In Savuti the war between these two predators seems to go in cycles, erupting into phases when you can hear one battle almost every night for weeks at a time. The excitement of watching these battles is intoxicating. On occasion I have rolled all the film out of the camera and, unable to hear that I was out of film, kept rolling away with an empty camera. Beverly and I have to touch each other to draw one another's attention to a piece of interesting action because even shouting is useless over the noise. The worst situation is when there are two carcasses and the battle ranges from one to the other. We then find ourselves moving the vehicle every few minutes because the action seems better at the other carcass or from a different angle.

Sometimes discoveries or ideas come in the most unusual ways and places. In Los Angeles while we edited the lion-hyena film *Eternal Enemies* with a fun team led by editor Barry Nye, we wrote the script for the film. At National Geographic, scripts are given a rigorous going-over, a process that, although it's painful at the time, we value greatly later when we have facts questioned by scientists and the public. At one script session, I was trying to explain the relationship between lions and hyenas. "Will one hyena take on a lion?" someone asked. No, both Beverly and I answered together.

"Four to one?"

"No!" I said. "It doesn't work like that at all. The number of hyenas in a clan and the number of lions in a pride probably keep the same proportions, but individual attitudes and events determine the interaction." Quite suddenly I had the idea to do a few calculations.

Back in an office with a view of a smoggy Hollywood mountain, I punched up some figures on the number of individuals in the clan compared to the number in the pride. The figures were very different. But when I calculated the weights of the hyenas and lions I arrived at something else. The total weight of the central pride was 4,050 pounds. The total weight of their associated hyena clan was 4,140 pounds. I went through some other estimated weights and clan-pride structures and found that in each case the total weight/mass of the clan very closely matched that of the pride of lions they most often competed with. The lion calculations all excluded males, and when males were added to the formula, the mass of the lions became much larger, which mirrored the behavior in the field: If male lions are added to the night's activity, the hyenas are overpowered and leave the area.

We first read about a male lion attacking a hyena in East Africa, an account by Hugo van Lawick and Jane Goodall in *Innocent Killers.* As we followed the male lions in Savuti we saw more examples of this, and a pattern started developing.

It began with Nyatsi.

One day while walking across an open area, he stopped and stared into a bush. It was midday. When he started stalking we thought a young impala might be hidden in the bushes. He ran into the thicket, and, after a confusion of squeals and growls and bushes and dust, the male lion emerged with a hyena.

Within a month we witnessed Tona and Nyatsi both actively hunt down hyenas. Then when the four new males took over, we saw one of the younger males, Cromwell, catch another hyena. Gradually we started finding hyena carcasses around more and more, but seldom did we see the same male

These three males, the Lions of Darkness, tilted the balance in the relationship between lions and hyenas in Savuti.

catch hyenas twice.

Then came Ntchwaidumela. He was one of the four challengers who ousted Tsididi, Tona, and Nyatsi, and he was the smallest of the new males, always noticeably more timid when it came to lion business such as mating the females or contesting any small point with his "brothers." In time the consortium broke up, and Mandevu, a dark-maned male, and the small Ntchwaidumela stayed in the south. They had the best territory in Savuti: the marsh.

Slowly we began to notice a change in Ntchwaidumela's behavior. One night as we trundled along behind the two males, the smaller one suddenly stopped, dropped his head down to shoulder height, and flattened his body into a crouching position as he glided forward, intent on something ahead that we couldn't see. We were not far from the hyena dens. He burst into a run, and after a 750-yard run he stopped, letting the hyena escape. With fire in his eyes he looked around, searching for another hyena that he saw lurking in the long grass. He charged again, another run of at least 500 yards. Then another broke cover and again he gave chase. All three escaped, but the male was obviously hunting them. Mandevu, the second male, just walked along in any direction Ntchwaidumela chose, not joining in the game.

Although he wasted a lot of effort that night, Ntchwaidumela chased hyena after hyena actively, trying to make contact until the area was cleared. Only then did the two males move on with their patrol. The young blonde male roared repeatedly after each chase. Ntchwaidumela—"the war greeting" or "he who greets with fire"—was christened that day. We saw this male chase hyenas many times over the five years we followed him. Soon he was no longer distinguishable as the "young" male, but he was always smaller than the other three he arrived with. Strangely, he was dominated by Mandevu, the dark companion, whenever an estrus female was around. Ntchwaidumela did get to spread his genes, but only if two females came into estrus at once.

One night we followed Tshaba's pride into a wildebeest hunt, not far from some hyena dens. Within minutes, the hyenas massed around them. Two kills had been made, and the hyenas very quickly grabbed one away. Tshaba's lionesses found themselves treed, watching the hyenas eat their kill. But a distant roar alerted the hyenas to a male lion's presence in the area. They ate quickly but nervously, and then, when they saw the male, they scattered. It was Mandevu. He came in casually, walked up to the kill, and started feeding. The hyenas must have known this lion by now. He had been in their area for nearly five years and they crossed each others' paths at least once a week.

Hyenas seem to have a great sense of the mood of a pride and even which lion is which. Some days they will trounce a whole pride of lions; other days one lioness is given a wide berth.

On this night, the hyenas gathered again as if to take over. The male lion turned and growled, enough to put off most hyena

A large carcass is hotly contested for days. Each night the possession of a kill can change from hyenas to lions, from one hyena clan to another and back, several times.

groups, but this was different. We had never seen Mandevu chase hyenas. The hyenas must have recognized something about this male, because hundreds of potential takeovers had dissolved into nothing with the arrival of Ntchwaidumela or the two males together.

The male lion was definitely in trouble when the full force of the clan combined to take back their kill. To our surprise, Mandevu got up and left. Quickly the hyenas swarmed in and claimed the kill, and one or two even raced up to Mandevu to see him off. With a token growl he trotted away, leaving most of the wildebeest to the hyenas.

The two questions about hyenas that are constantly on our minds are: What is it about hyenas that turns them into a frenzied mob of such tremendous efficiency? and, Why does it happen?

One possible theory is that when their ancestors, the huge sociable hyenas, fed on the ancient savannas of Africa with the saber-toothed lions, the two animals had very distinct roles. The saber-tooths were hunters, killing by ambushing and using their powerful bodies and in particular their teeth to rip into the flesh of victims. (Most of the victims were large then too.) These weapons were efficient for killing, but not terribly efficient for feeding, because they got caught on the bones and meat of the prey. As a result, ancestral lions left behind huge quantities of meat, probably more than 50 percent of their kills. The sociable hyenas simply filled that role of scavenging and cleaning up the remains.

But things change, and the Darwinian theory of natural selection favored the smaller-toothed of these saber-toothed lions, maybe because of a need to catch smaller prey and feed on them, or simply because there is an evolutionary advantage in being efficient. Those that wasted got less and faded away, leaving the stronger, smaller-toothed versions to dominate breeding. Among the hyenas, too, the smaller models survived better, but now the lions were feeding on more of the carcasses, eating greater proportions of the meat, and leaving much less for the hyenas.

The hyenas were forced to adapt. To get food they had to compete with the lions for the carcasses, an environment and natural food supply they knew well, and they also had to begin hunting their own prey in competition with the lions. They banded together into larger groups to even the score. Because these two species now compete for the same food supply and more often for the very same carcass, the sound of hyenas feeding now attracts lions, who must associate feeding with the sound, and vice versa.

Somehow we got caught up in the middle of this evolution. When we, in our ancestral form of *Australopithecus,* hid in our caves, our natural predator was a leopard-like creature called *Dinofelis.* As the saber-tooths and the sociable hyenas drew closer together in their feeding niche, *Dinofelis* got squeezed out between them, slipping away into extinction. This was a mixed blessing for us, because now we had to contend with two predators: lions and

In the southern marsh hyenas race in the instant a kill is made. While one threatens the lioness from behind, others of the clan wrest the kill away from under her nose.

Hyenas, often derided as mere scavengers, kill substantial numbers of prey. It is not unusual for their kills to be stolen from them by hungry lions.

hyenas. No doubt this accounts somewhat for our present-day attitudes toward these two animals. But the difference between our innate feelings about the two species is still hard to fathom.

Throughout Europe and other parts of the world, lion statues adorn almost every city, town, or hamlet. You will see them as door knockers in Venice or huge statues in Trafalgar square. But never have we seen a hyena symbolized in stone, paint, or even plastic!

Ntchwaidumela shared mankind's hatred of hyenas.

The rains had started and zebra were in the marsh. We had lions for the night, but just after sunset they walked east into the forest of mopane and we were left behind, not wanting to brave the dense scrub and the certainty of punctured tires. On nights like this we drive, looking for any sign of either other lions or hyenas that we can sit with in the hope that they might lead us to something interesting. We found Mandevu in the middle of the marsh, roaring half-heartedly from time to time. After an hour with him we saw him look up into the dark in anticipation of something. We shone around and saw the unmistakable sight of a small male with a big blonde mane. Ntchwaidumela. He walked in with a determined stride and greeted Mandevu. These two males, unlike their predecessors, seldom spent much time showing affection to each other. They rubbed heads briefly and separated and lay down a few lion lengths apart.

For the next half hour they were both silent, looking around into a blackness in which we could see nothing.

Over a mile away, the zebra stampeded. Both males looked toward the noise but did not bother to get up. Then we all heard the hyenas. They had chased and killed a zebra foal; the cries of the foal mingled with the sounds of hyena cackles. Ntchwaidumela reacted immediately, jumping up and trotting off in the direction of the noise. We knew what was coming. We raced around ahead of him to get into position but had to stop twice to get a direction fix on the noises. As we pulled up at the kill Beverly saw Ntchwaidumela next to us—he had covered the distance as fast as we had. The lights went on and the camera rolled as the male charged in, landing on the most dominant hyena, biting into her shoulder, rolling over and ripping with his back legs. He adjusted his mouthhold and sank his teeth into her back, forcing his jaws closed. We heard the bones crack. The way he shook the hyena was like no other kill we've seen. It was a definite attempt to break every bone in the victim's body. "Fury" and "rage" are the best adjectives for what we were seeing. Within seconds other hyenas gathered and counterattacked the male, biting his rump hard enough to make him release his hold on the matriarch but not enough to quell his apparent rage, because he lashed out and raced after them. The matriarch we found later, with a broken back.

Ntchwaidumela had become the "hyena killer."

Filming this interaction, the most difficult lion behavior to follow and film because it happens so spontaneously and sporadically, came as a relief rather than a reward. Just a few months before we'd had a screening of a rough edit of our film *Eternal Enemies* for the executives of National Geographic. They liked it, but after we finished, Tom Simon, a good friend and the executive producer, asked what the ultimate hyena-lion interaction was. We said that a male lion attacking a hyena was probably the most dramatic. "Do you have the actual contact?" he asked. "No," we said. "But we'll get it." Then Tom asked us how many times in ten years we'd seen such behavior, to which we had to reply, "Not often." "Good luck!" was all he could say.

Now we had it. But Beverly still didn't have the photographs, as she was working filming lights and doing sound. Everything happened too fast to do too many jobs.

Just a month later we were following the females of Maome's pride. It was Christmas Eve, and despite invitations from Lloyd Wilmot to join them in their Savuti camp for a meal, we declined. It was to be a quiet Christmas Eve for us, alone on the marsh with the lions.

That night, Tshaba's pride and Maome's pride clashed over some zebra. Maome's pride ended up with the carcasses, and the rest of Christmas Eve was fairly peaceful. By 2:00 a.m., like many other people in the world, we lay down to rest. Unlike others, we slept among lions feeding on zebra, the crunching of bones and growling lulling us to sleep.

The morning was crisp and clear. The marsh grasses were patches of winter brown and summer green. A few clouds were heading our way from the south, and the lions, as well as any sign of the zebra, had gone. Three hyenas nosed around, and one or two jackals squabbled in the grass over some hidden fragments, the last clue that a massacre had taken place here.

From the top of the marsh, Mandevu roared. Although she was well over five miles away, one of the hyenas looked up, raised her tail, and loped off in that direction. We were keen to follow because we were beginning to suspect the female hyena of being the new matriarch of the marsh clan, a successor after Ntchwaidumela dispatched the last matriarch. It was a surprisingly short transition period, by our experience. Most times when rendered leaderless the clan is totally disrupted, even disbanding if no obvious matriarch emerges. The fallen matriarch's cubs lose all rank and sometimes wander around aimlessly in and out of the territory, as had been the case with this clan only a month before.

Especially because of the clan's weak state now, the scene we witnessed next was a bit of a surprise.

The female hyena found the lion. It wasn't difficult—he was walking south down the center of the marsh, roaring every ten minutes. He was obviously looking for the pride because he sniffed constantly, and we could see lion tracks on the path ahead of him. During the day hyenas usually give lions a wide berth, in particular if there is no sign of food about. But on this day, Christmas 1990, the hyena actively sought out the male lion and then started harassing him. All previous cases we'd seen of lion-hyena interactions initiated by hyenas had been when hyenas were heavily favored by their numbers. This was a one-on-one conflict.

The male lion started to mark by urinating and scraping his back legs over the urine in the dirt. By all definitions this is a territorial display. Textbooks tell us that territories are like glass spheres, invisible to all but those who are of the same species and can see or smell these boundaries. Jackals, hyenas, lions, wildebeests, African wildcats, servals, mice, snakes, and a host of other animals may all have territories on the same piece of land with different boundaries, all invisible to one another but obvious to others of their own species.

Now the lion was marking aggressively across the species barrier, and, amazingly, as he moved off, the matriarchal hyena raced up to that spot and deposited her own mark on top of his. This apparently infuriated the lion, and he charged, but the hyena ran away, circled, and started her harassment again. We tried to figure out what was going on. If there had been dens in the area, we would have been less puzzled but still amazed by the hyena's confidence. If there had been food around it would have provided a partial explanation for the behavior. Neither was the case.

This hyena was badgering the male, and because it was Mandevu he didn't retaliate.

Ntchwaidumela, the hyena killer.

In fact, he was soon losing ground, walking faster and with less grace. His ears were flat against his head and his posture was that of a young submissive lion rather than a pride male.

The hyena's growling and whooping attracted other hyenas, and soon there were five clan members around. They looked as confused as we were, but they did participate a little. Just as Mandevu was about to break into a run, which would have been terribly undignified, in broad daylight with a handful of hyenas seeing him off, one hyena noticed the lionesses of Maome's pride walking in from the west. Their heads were held high, making them look bigger and fatter in the neck, their body postures exuding aggression. A low babble ran among the hyenas as a warning, but the matriarch took a quick look and resumed her harassment of Mandevu. As the lionesses approached, two gave chase to the hyenas on the outskirts of the field and gave up.

Then, in the far distance, we saw Ntchwaidumela coming at a fast, steady pace. He had heard the sounds of the skirmish, and from the looks of him, he was about to turn it into a battle. Mandevu lay down. The matriarch circled him and marked again and made off just before Motsumi saw what was happening and chased. Ntchwaidumela broke into a full run, a charge from 150 yards or more, his mouth agape, sucking air down his throat, pumping oxygen into his lungs, fueling his heart. As soon as he was close enough for us to see his eyes, we could discern the fixed direction of his gaze. It was on the matriarch, and for the full run those yellow eyes never left their target.

The matriarch's back legs reached in front of the front feet as if her rear end was determined to outrun her front. Motsumi was in full swing right behind that rear end and swiped out, hooking a lazy back leg. The matriarch tumbled, swinging around in a full flying circle, crying out in alarm, exposing her only defense: her teeth. Motsumi pulled back and the hyena righted herself in full fall, picking up her footing like a gymnast and racing for the hills. Ntchwaidumela didn't falter. His gait just stretched longer and longer, reaching for the hyena. The gap closed slowly. The hyena looked over her shoulder, saw the lion, and put a final effort into her escape. But the male lion pulled from his own reserves of energy, and the gap closed just a little bit more. When the time was right, Ntchwaidumela reached forward first with one paw and then the other and latched on to the legs of the hyena. The speed of the chase carried on its momentum, taking both the lion and the hyena skidding along the ground. As they skidded, the male moved his grip up the hyena's back, positioning his head for the killing bite to the neck. The growls and hyena squeals faded away with the life of the hyena, until all was silent and the hyena lay still. It was Christmas day, and we were exhausted by 7:30 in the morning. We had our gift for the season. This was the footage we needed to prove that Ntchwaidumela's hatred for hyenas was absolute and individual.

Anyone who watches a violent contact between lions and hyenas, one that is not related to food, can see plainly that there is a blood feud running between them that is uncannily similar to those at which our own species is so adept. I think that's what people find so disturbing about this relationship. The idea that "enemies" can exist in nature is hard for some to swallow. Scientists say that these animals cannot experience the equivalent of human emotions such as compassion, fear, sadness, hatred, and anger. And yet, even while the logical half of my brain scorns the notion, the same half says, "Yes, what you see are exactly those five emotions." Are emotions so dear to us that we think we have exclusive rights to them?

We have seen the signs that tell us lions are feeling compassion, hatred, fear, anger, and sadness. The lioness coming back to her dying cub time after time. The pride accepting the old male lion Sequela after years of separation, when another pride would have chased him off, as the original challenging males had two years before. A lion who specializes in chasing and killing hyenas, who in fact goes to extraordinary lengths to kill them, but doesn't eat them. The daily greeting ritual, mutual grooming, lying together, calling for each other, the running and playing: all of the above tells us that if we weren't bogged down in our extreme desire to avoid giving "human" sentiments to animals, we could accept these examples as proof of simple emotions and get on with the work of exploring these emotions further.

Hyenas try to circle and distract lionesses during confrontations. The clan drives itself into a frenzy with aggressive "takeover" calls.

The hyenas' audacity and aggressiveness are directly proportional to their numerical superiority in confrontations with lions. For the lions, one tactic of defense is to keep facing the hyenas. When hyenas manage to maneuver behind lions, they can inflict serious wounds. Such interactions can leave the whole pride bleeding and shaken for days.

Whether quarreling over food or territory, or out of sheer mutual dislike, in Savuti lions and hyenas attack each other on sight.

Ntchwaidumela was relentless in his attacks on hyenas. Each time he seemed to take pleasure in biting down hard and deep until bones cracked.

LEARNING FROM THE LIONS

We have seen lions come and go over the decade. We will remember them all. Each one was a different character and each one had a different face. The lioness with the curious face and furrowed brow who turned her head slowly from side to side when looking at us. The one with an unmistakably beautiful face—and the band of long-faced lionesses from Tshaba's pride. The males are always easy to identify by the color, size, and shape of their mane.

In Savuti there is a natural flow of male lions. They appear to come in from the south or southwest, up through the marsh. Then they work their way north, acquiring territories along the way by ousting older males. Finally, after a few years, they seem to tire of Savuti and venture west. Since 1981, every male still holding a territory has disappeared to the west. For years we puzzled over this phenomenon, and in the mid-eighties we decided to investigate.

To the west the last waters of the Savuti attracted large groups of animals, supporting the buffalo herds and zebra migrations in the dry months. It was a lion paradise. But lions cannot simply migrate to the best food supply; they are locked into a territory system, similar to the one that prevents people from wandering from house to house. When animals move, they go from one lion territory to the next, along and through a network or chain of territories. The only reason a male lion might follow would be if the territories were vacant. In this case, the reason for vacancy was clear. The land adjoining the Savuti section of the Chobe National Park was a government-sanctioned hunting concession. Here safari hunters from around the world came to hunt animals for sport. After well over a decade of shooting male lions, at an average of 10 to 15 lions shot per year, almost 200 male lions had left the area as trophies. We were beginning to notice the effect of this continuous harvesting of male lions on all the lions in northern Botswana.

In just ten years in Savuti, all but one of the male lions we studied were eventually taken by trophy hunters. Rautang, Jansen, Lyall, Matabula, Quedi, Sama, Olsen, Tona, Tsididi, Nyatsi, Mabala, Cromwell, and even the long-reigning Mandevu and his brother Ntchwaidumela, the great hyena killer. I know that wherever Ntchwaidumela's skin hangs, on a wall somewhere in the U.S.A., perhaps, the new owners have no idea of the life that this lion lived. The daily heroics, the matings, the battles with elephant and buffalo, and, of course, his almost nightly vendettas against hyenas can never be seen on his fading skin. The continuous shooting of resident males had created a vacuum, and these lions had filled it. The vacuum is then maintained because the largest lions in the area are the new arrivals from Savuti, and of course, largely because of our own work, these lions are very accustomed to vehicles and get shot immediately.

Even the above situation, in and of itself, is not disastrous, although it effectively means that for every male lion shot, between five and fourteen lions actually die. Lions have an amazing reproductive system that allows space for massive die-offs. Each lioness has an average of two cubs every two years for about ten years. A pride can easily cast out a group of six sub-adults every three years, most of whom die simply because there is no place for them in the tightly formed mosaic of lion territories. From this group of outcasts, however, the genetic strains of the dominant pride male are passed on through the sub-adult males, some of whom will surface again somewhere to take over a pride. This prevents the lion community from inbreeding.

But in the Linyanti and Selinda area (the hunting concessions adjoining Savuti), the depletion of good quality male lions who would have occupied and bred successfully in the prime riverfront territories (A-grade lions) left vacuums for B-graders, who were also shot. It is difficult to tell exactly how far down the alphabet of quality we have come now, but we got a good indication between 1990 and 1994, which I'll get to in a moment. When we surveyed the area in 1983 we saw 17 male lions in a three-day period. Hunters reported "many lions to choose from." But by 1990 the effects of the hunting were beginning to show throughout northern Botswana.

The females in the hunting concession, who are relatively immune to the hunters, are bombarded by incoming males, ready to spread their goodwill in the male vacuum, every year. Most still have cubs from last season's trophy male, so, because it is the way of lions, the incoming male immediately hunts down and kills her cubs. On this basis, our figure for actual lion deaths in the area over ten years is 3,000!

Besides the fact that when we started our work in Savuti we identified seven pride males and today there are two, the indication that lions are being depleted comes from the pride around our new camp in Zibadianja, in the hunting concession. Here a pride of lions started with two females. When they were mated, a professional hunter drove up to them and shot the male from the female's back during a copulation, in what was the most despicable display of bad taste exhibited so far. Ironically, the mating was a success, and six cubs were born. Three were young, adventurous

The hippo killers of Zibadianja became very accustomed to our presence.
They wandered freely amongst our tents day and night, even killing a hippo right in camp.

males. By the time they were 2½ years old, no new males remained in the area at all. We searched constantly, and each time we caught a glimpse of even a nomadic subadult of four years, he would appear within days on the back of a hunter's pickup, headed for the skinning shed. We had basically moved down the alphabet of territory grades.

By three years of age the small cubs still moved with their sisters and the two mothers. Then slowly we started to find the pride with odd females missing. Their fragmentation was explained by the appearance of one of the mothers in full lactation, indicating that she had just given birth to new cubs, and later the same day we witnessed the surprise mating of one of the female cubs by one of her brothers. The three males mated with their sisters and their mothers! Fourteen cubs were born.

By now we had begun to plead with the hunters to back off. We had spoken to the wildlife department and conservation agencies, but all had said that we needed more hard evidence. The hunters themselves admitted privately that it was almost impossible to find a trophy lion to shoot, which should have told everyone something, but publicly they denounced us as "bunny huggers."

Finally we spoke to all the hunters who might come across the local pride and explained the structure and the situation of the young males, who, at 3½, were obviously at least 3 years away from trophy size. Within days of the opening of the 1994 hunting season, two of these males were shot. At the time they were so used to vehicles, having grown up with our vehicle and those of a new tourist camp at Selinda, that shooting them must have been a great disappointment to the hunting client.

Just before the season started, all three males had come through our camp and spray marked against our solar panel, which was balanced against a bush. Every day for a month after his two brothers were shot, the last young male came to the solar panel and smelled it, moaning softly. He joined them a month later, and the roaring around our camp went silent for over a year.

Soon the males of the group of 14 cubs will be old enough to mate with their sisters, their mothers, and their grandmothers.

As alarming as all of this is, both personally and from an environmental standpoint, it is just one example in a system. We don't know about the other lions in Botswana. How many systems are having their lion populations slowly eroded? How many other species, like the zebra, for example, are under the same slow pressure? And while our attention is focused on lions and even more so on elephants, pandas, and whales, what about the slow and steady rot that has set in behind the scenes, a cancer of wildlife and the African wilderness, that can't really be blamed on anyone? Hunters do what they are allowed to do and are often ignorant of the intricacies of the systems they hunt. Governments in Africa are doing what they think is right for their people. But the reality is that almost all of our current attitudes toward wildlife are based on inherited colonial extravagancies and elitisms.

No serious conservationist could condemn Frederick Courtenay Selous for his

Between migrations the savanna can be a desolate place for predators locked into a territorial system that prevents them from following the herds.

hunting of African "Big Game" a hundred years ago. But times have changed. Now there is not enough to go around, and we have to review our relationship with wildlife and wilderness. It was once so precious that we wanted to collect it; now it is even more precious and more rare. Can we allow ourselves the luxury of letting it stay the way it is? To many this is sacrilege. Wildlife, they argue, should be used—it is either meat or dangerous. Those same critics see wilderness as a quality of the western mind, an expensive fantasy that the rest of the world pays for with its abstinence.

It is difficult to fully understand the attitudes of a well fed, wealthy hunter from another land who travels to Africa and pays to be driven up to a sleepy lion in order to shoot it as a trophy. The act of hunting is said to have ancestral roots, but whatever happened to the notion of facing down one's fate by staring into the eyes of your enemy? Many lions in Botswana are shot from vehicles, not so much for safety but because, I'm told by the guides, 90 percent of the hunters have difficulty getting in and out of a truck, let alone walking behind a lion in the September heat for a few hours. This symbolic emasculation of our most feared and respected animal enemy is now, for the most part, being carried out by the most unlikely people, warriors devoid of nobility or any sense of dignity.

The future for lions? The death of the three young males in the Selinda area came as Beverly and I were lobbying hard for a moment of sanity in the hunting world, and it proved the issue. After numerous articles and presentations to the ministers and the president of Botswana, the long awaited changes started to happen. The hunters lost the concessions, and the photographic tourism industry won the land. In 1994 the number of lions licensed to be shot was 100; the next year, the quota was cut to 8 for the whole country. Attitudes toward hunting, and in particular the hunting of lions in Botswana, have begun to change.

Although it was emotionally costly at the time, I'm pleased that we had something to do with that change. One can only study an animal's behavior for so long before feeling compelled to delve further into its survival and, ultimately, the politics that surround it, even though to do so takes the focus off one's work as an animal behaviorist, photographer, or filmmaker. Without advocates, who would speak on behalf of these various species? The passion to speak out has its roots in the appreciation of all that is Africa, human and animal.

For many, the knowledge that somewhere there is a vast wilderness with animals like lions that will eat you if you give them the chance will always be a comfort. Without that knowledge, the soul may not die of a great loneliness, as the often misquoted Chief Seattle put it, but it will wither of a great boredom, knowing that all the unknown and potentially dangerous places have been tamed.

In a few years this rear neck bite will be perfect for bringing down a zebra or a buffalo.

It is difficult to accept that all lion behavior can be explained in coldly scientific terms; that "enjoyment," "compassion," and "hatred" are "anthropomorphisms" and inaccurate as descriptions of lion behavior. We believe that there is much to be learned about the emotions of animals in the wild.

Zibadianja can be as fruitful as Savuti once was, if left untouched by hunters.

EPILOGUE

We still keep up with the lions of Savuti. We always ask ourselves why we don't go back to live in Savuti permanently with the lions, but we have found our own sanctuary even further away from people. In isolation here we can concentrate on the work that needs silence and no disturbances. We still work in Savuti for months each year, and live out of our vehicle. It's all we need.

In our absence, the members of Lloyd Wilmot's camp staff maintain meticulous records of lion sightings and share our passion for these prides and the area. Before we start work there each time, we spend a few hours catching up on all the gossip of the lion world with them. They have introduced us to a new pride, the Setari pride, so named because of a rather peculiar affinity for trees and tree climbing.

While new prides and prospects are erupting, the past slowly changes. It is generally believed that prides of lions continue even though individuals die with each generation. But over the years we have seen lion prides disappear: Dingala's pride, Ludo's pride, even Tshaba's pride, and others have simply run out of productive energy. Just as the breath slowly ebbs from the beast that is Savuti, so it seems it can drain from a pride of lions.

Watching Maome's pride fade away was both disturbing and scientifically compelling, especially because we saw them emerge as young subadults and form a group. By the end of 1994 Maome was just a stick figure. Motsumi was little better. All the other lionesses were thin but still healthy. Earlier in the year Smudge had died. A dislocated shoulder necessitated her being shot. Lloyd and the game scouts went out to dispatch her one sad morning when we weren't in Savuti.

The buffalo moved through Savuti late in December. Maome's pride struggled to keep up and finally brought down a calf. It was down for 15 minutes before the rest of the buffalo herd returned, chased the lions away, and rescued their calf. While we were wondering if the calf would survive, we heard the bellows of a dying buffalo cow. The younger females of Maome's pride wrestled the old cow to the ground just as the first hyenas came running in. It was 10:00 p.m. From then on throughout the night the battle for the carcass raged on. Most of the lionesses were seriously bitten and chased up trees. Maome and Motsumi were too old to run in fear and stayed on their kill regardless of the marauders around them. Twice we saw Maome's skin being stripped off her back. Motsumi leaped up in the air, growling as a hyena sunk its teeth into her back leg.

By dawn the carcass was a blood spot in the grass. Maome's pride limped off to the edge of the marsh, each female bleeding from a wound. Maome lagged behind by a half an hour's walk.

Two days later the buffalo returned. The thin lions had full bellies but no more flesh on their bones. We knew they were dying, dying of old age and broken spirits. Motsumi finally mustered the energy to walk into the thicket behind the buffalo. Two other lionesses limped in after her. Maome and the pride's one cub waited in the shade, hidden from the half moonlight. We waited as well, convinced that if we left her we would never see her again. It was the 28th of December.

A buffalo bellowed, a sound we knew well as a direct hit by a lion, then bushes cracked and lions ran in the dust about 200 yards from us. We resisted the urge to investigate. More bellows, then lion growls, bellows, then guttural moans.

After an hour we moved in. The buffalo had clearly gone, and we couldn't hear a kill. Maome hadn't responded either.

Just after dawn we searched around again and a vulture gave away the position of the kill. The bird glided down past the hauntingly stark trees that typify Savuti and all its harshness, and onto the bloodied body of Motsumi. A buffalo, not a hyena, had been her end. Two days later Maome disappeared from the pride and, just in case, we followed no more vultures that week.

Four females and one two-year-old cub remain, all thin and struggling toward similar fates. The real question now is, is this really the end of a pride of lions? If yes, then it is the end of what is probably the most documented lion pride, one we observed from its inception, with the split of Maome from her mother's pride in the early eighties. The beginning and the end. It is unusual for Africa and its myths, but there will be no more beginnings, at least for this pride, just the tin trunks full of dusty photographs and daily observations and volumes of memories that drift about without chronology in our minds, prompted by the sight of an old tree or water hole where some grand battle was once fought or some tender moment shared.

At our camp in Zibadianja we have all our editing equipment for the film work we do. We keep the little that we have in worldly possessions there, and we have lions. Just recently we followed the subadults as they tried to hunt in the valley behind camp. The females did most of the work; the young males, now just about two years old, were as stupid about hunting as every two-year-old is. They failed on the zebra and the giraffe attempts. By then they were within sight of our camp,

Maome and her pride lost the battle against time. No one will know the glory and hardship, the play, the challenges, the defeats seen through those amber eyes.

and the moon came up—hunting was over. They had at least learned about hunting with the moon. But play was still in progress.

We went ahead to camp, made a fire, and warmed the meal we were planning to have. Soon the lechwe ran into the water and called, a sure sign that predators were on their way. With a torch we could see their eyes approaching us. We waited around the fire, and it was the oldest young male that we saw first in the firelight, watching us from about 20 yards. When he saw a movement he ducked away to his left, and I knew what he was up to. Beside the fire an anthill hid us from the north wind; he was going to use that for cover to circle around us. I crept onto the anthill and waited as he looked around at the fire—I was three feet away. He bolted away, back to the firewood pile where he'd been at first. By the time he got there, Beverly was at the firewood pile. He bounded back to the anthill and feigned surprise when he saw me. It was all a game. Subadults are always great for a game.

We are getting to know these lions now. One day, we hope, we will piece together a chart of all the lion territories in northern Botswana and more of the puzzle will fall into place.

For us here in our new camp at Zibadianja, the lions provide an ever surprising glimpse into lion behavior. The pride of incestuous notoriety has developed an ability and taste for hunting a very different kind of prey. While on the hunt, the youngsters play a game we call "surfing."

Moving in a giant, flat parabola through the grass, one young lioness surreptitiously cuts off a hippo's only route to water. The young males are busy stalking straight in toward the huge fat rump of the hippo, whose only reaction to all this is an incessant munching of grass. Slow steps match the up and down head movement as the pachyderm chomps away at the grass underfoot.

By now two young females are lying in wait between the peaceful hippo and the water's edge. Way back across the floodplain we can still see the two adult females, these subadult lions' mothers. Try as they might they cannot control their grown cubs now, and they watch aloofly from a little island of palm trees, not participating at all, but not ready to leave the cubs to their own devices.

The game is on. The hippo snorts out in alarm, swings around with an agility more befitting a much smaller animal, and faces the creeping lions. Two males are in place and they flatten themselves into the grass, but their efforts are still clumsy and the hippo locates them easily. He charges, roaring and snorting like the overgrown pig that he is. Saliva dribbles from his pink open mouth.

Then the hippo turns and starts a direct but slow walk toward water and the two waiting female cubs. This is exactly what the two young males want, and they immediately run in at the swaying rump of the hippo. The hippo runs, but one young male is on him, front paws clutching the back, back paws still running along the ground behind the hippo. The lion makes no attempt to bite the hippo but from his elevated position takes the opportunity to look around (proudly!) at the other lions. He tries to dig his back feet into the turf that is now beginning to get wetter as they approach the river. Suddenly the two female cubs are up. It is a good ambush, or would be if the prey were something a little less like a steamroller. The hippo, now bellowing and growling fiercely, barges his way through the lionesses. One lioness jumps out of the way, but ducks around to join the young male riding behind. She can only get one paw on, so she runs on her back legs like her brother but keeps the other front paw out at an angle to keep balance. She looks exactly like a young surfer, performing a perfect "hang ten."

The other cubs all run along behind, looking for an opportunity to join in, but the ride is almost over. The hippo and his two travelling companions have reached the river. The hippo splashes in eagerly, and as the lions feel the water around them they leap off their courier, jumping awkwardly into the shallow muddy water that even in the moonlight stains their golden skins.

The hippo has gone into the reeds, calling a gruff *Ha, ha, ha, ha* in the shallows, and the cubs all get together, rub heads, roll on top of each other, and lick one another's faces. The two mothers haven't moved.

The cubs get up to return to their mothers and start to run and ambush one another, playing cub games. Suddenly a young male stops, looks out into the darkness, and sees the dark shape of a hippo snuffling along, munch-

Flicking water from her tail, a young lioness overcomes her aversion to water to feed on a bull elephant.

ing as he goes. All the cubs follow his gaze and respond. We set our cameras, check how much film we have loaded, and get ready, because we know "surf's up."

The future for us in this field is an exciting labyrinth of discovery and communication. So much research knowledge is locked away from everyone, and this isolation of science is what breeds myth and misconception. Our role is to banish those myths and explain the misconceptions. Africa has more than its share of both, and, surprisingly, it is mysterious not only to outsiders but to Africans as well. We may be able to move the barriers to understanding just a little: That is our ambition.

We have spent a great deal of time with elephants as well, working on a film called *Reflections on Elephants* and trying to understand just a little more about them, searching always for a clue to what makes them what they are. Only through constant testing of our knowledge can we hope to catch the slightest glimmer of something new.

Experimenting in iridology (a technique based on the idea that patterns in the iris of the eye relate to health in different parts of the body), Beverly has begun to photograph the eyes of lions and elephants we know. With our knowledge of the health of each animal, we look for correlations between the patterns in their eyes and any injuries or illnesses the animals have. We are also experimenting with recordings of lions we have made over the years to find out more about their voice patterns as they grow older. There are a lot of exciting projects ahead for us. We can't wait.

There are characteristics of the bush that strike me as essential and symbolic, not just of the bush but of Africa itself; some of these are my favorite things in the world. The feeling of having lions close by, the smell of the wild sage, the smell of elephants—the slightly acidic, earthy smell of their urine and dung that lingers after their departure from the water hole. The same musty smell of their skins up close, and the most comforting sound in the world: gentle elephant rumbles of communication. The racing chaotic panorama of zebra stripes in a big herd, and the dancing flocks of quelea birds as they sway and break away not as individual birds but as one flock made up of millions. The arrogant expression of the sable antelope bull, and the unparalleled grace with which the huge eland carries its bulk as it runs to the water hole to drink. The distant coughing of a leopard that we will more than likely never see, and the soft groan of a lioness as she calls her companions.

With all this energy around us, it is difficult for me to believe that it isn't somehow saturating everything on a cosmic level, impossible to believe that it could one day all just fade away and become a ghostly whisper, caught only for a moment on a brittle piece of film or between the dusty covers of a book.

Is it possible that this is the last place in all time and space where the elephants will rumble and the great flocks of quelea will dance? Are these the last shapes to slither through the silver grass, from the dappled shade of one tree to the next, hunting with the moon?

As we struggle to preserve the earth, to ensure that the wondrous pleasures upon which our eyes and minds feast will dance on like the great quelea flocks of Botswana, we gain insights into our own lonely souls.

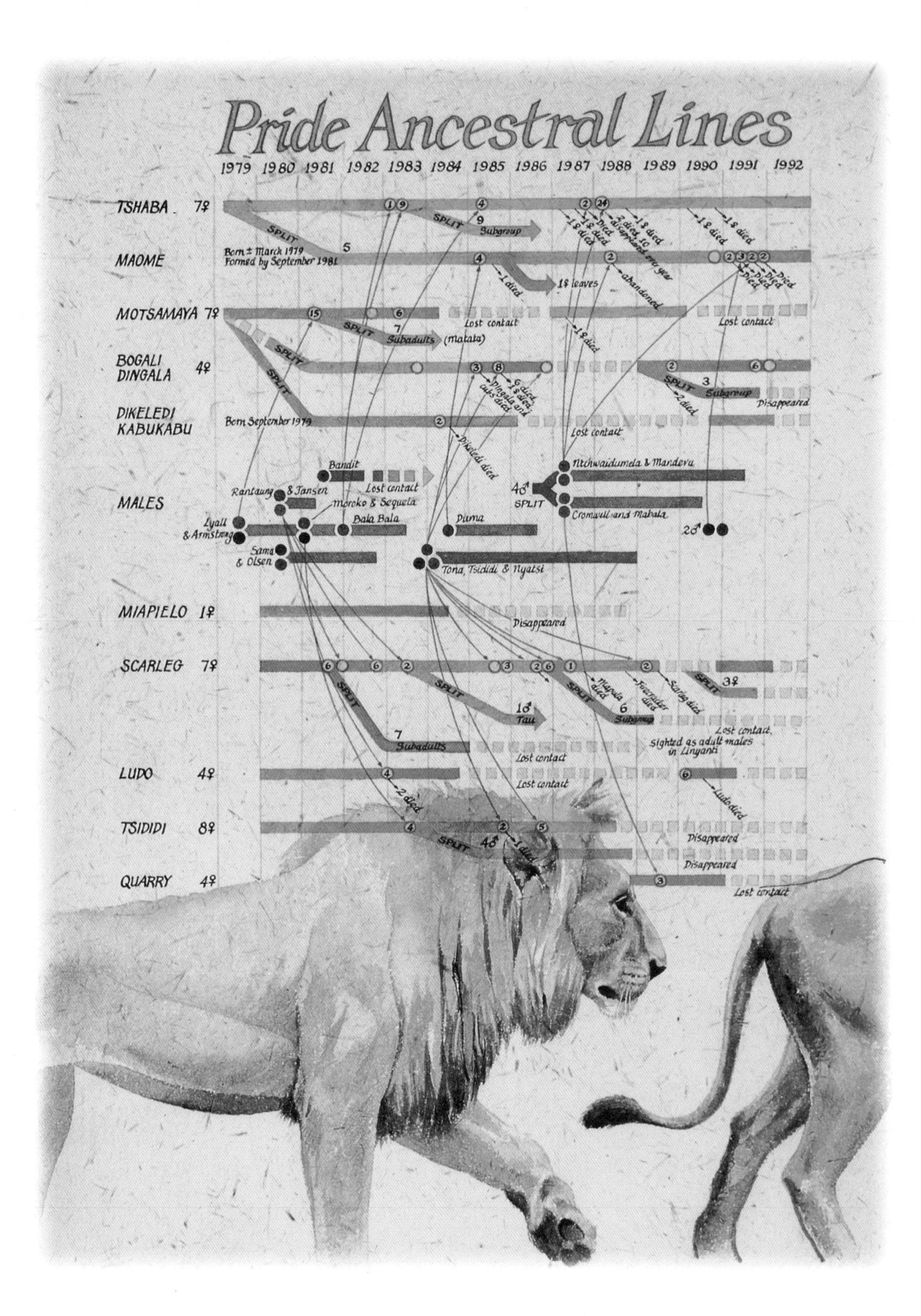
Pride Ancestral Lines
1979 1980 1981 1982 1983 1984 1985 1986 1987 1988 1989 1990 1991 1992
TSHABA 7♀
SPLIT
Subgroup
MAOME
Born ± March 1979
Formed by September 1981
1♀ leaves
abandoned
MOTSAMAYA 7♀
Subadults (Matata)
Lost contact
BOGALI DINGALA 4♀
Subgroup
Disappeared
DIKELEDI KABUKABU
Born September 1979
Dikeledi died
MALES
Bandit
Rantaung & Jansen
Moroko & Sequela
Lyall & Armstrong
Bala Bala
Sama & Olsen
Puma
Tona, Tsididi & Nyatsi
Nthwaidumela & Mandevu
Cromwell and Mahala
MIAPIELO 1♀
Disappeared
SCARLEG 7♀
Tau
Subgroup
Subadults
Sighted as adult males in Linyanti
LUDO 4♀
Ludo died
TSIDIDI 8♀
QUARRY 4♀
Lost contact